Praise for Sell Like a Team

"Successful selling is no longer about singular displays of proficiency by sole practitioners. The buying landscape has fundamentally shifted to one where committees today define needs and make decisions. Consequently the modern seller, to be successful, must learn how to create, organize, rehearse, and execute with a team that works perfectly in unison, if he or she is to win. In his book *Sell Like a Team*, Michael Dalis provides timely, insightful, and practical approaches for effective team selling that are critically needed in today's complex selling environment."

—John Elsey, President and CEO,
The Richardson Company

"*Sell Like a Team* is a must-read for all sales leaders. Michael Dalis combines his strategic vision and sales experience to provide a process for sales teams to use for winning results. He shares sales examples we all can relate to. In our complex world, where teams of employees work remotely, in different business units, and in different offices, Michael offers a step-by-step process that enables teams to align and effectively sell together. In the commercial insurance arena, teams of underwriting, claims, sales, and loss control will have greater success when they follow the sales strategies outlined in *Sell Like a Team*. My only disappointment is that he didn't write the book 10 years ago!"

—Ann Zaprazny, Senior Vice President,
Erie Insurance

"In the world of complex B2B selling at the enterprise level, selling has become a team sport. So many sales reps struggle to marshal internal resources, align with the buying team, and play the role of 'orchestra conductor' effectively, to lead great meetings and move deals forward. That said, if you're going to listen to someone's advice to improve your team selling approach, you're in good hands with Michael Dalis. I know. I've worked with Michael; I've hired Michael. Pull up a chair and get ready to think about what makes great teams great—in memorable, actionable ways that you can use to improve your sales results."

—Mike Kunkle, Sales Transformation Strategist,
TransformingSalesResults.com

"Teamwork is essential in the wealth management space. As families have grown more complex, it's gotten trickier to engage them effectively. A few years ago, I was fortunate to have Michael work with teams of my investment professionals on this type of team-based sales process. My folks were so fired up that word spread to the other professional disciplines across the wealth management business of our major bank. These principles allowed our portfolio managers to become leaders within their wealth management teams and those teams to work more effectively so that we could both deliver on client expectations and drive results for the bank."

—Tim Leach, Chief Investment Officer (Retired),
U.S. Bank Wealth Management

"Creating a team to win a high-stakes sales meeting, whether that means advancing or closing a deal, is more complex than most sales leaders and salespeople realize. Michael has not only done it successfully himself, he uses stories and academic research to break down the process into parts that sales professionals at all experience levels can implement. *Sell Like a Team* is not only a great read, buying and using this book is short money in that it will help you and your teams win more and win big."

—Bob Terson, author of *Selling Fearlessly*

"Business-to-business relationships have changed significantly over the last 10 years to where the buying decision is diffused across many stakeholders. *Sell Like a Team* masterfully guides the reader through the sales orchestration process critical to winning in complex sales cycles."

—Irv Grossman, Executive VP, Americas,
CHAINalytics

"In technology sales, the number of moving parts can be overwhelming. Selling teams are often geographically dispersed, as well as overscheduled. Subject matter experts, implementation teams, customer support reps, executives, partner firms, legal representatives—the list of participants in any one deal can go on and on. Michael provides a clear, logical, and easily mastered approach to team selling that will reduce both the time and complexity associated with working together successfully and will lead to winning more business."

—Kelley Dunn, VP of Outside Sales,
SambaSafety

"As a senior leader in the investment management business, I send our very talented people out every day to earn clients' trust, grow relationships, and win new engagements. The challenges are that clients are well informed and have many choices in advisers, all smart, qualified, and professional. My team must be able to answer the "Why us?" question. Bullet points in a presentation won't do it, it's how our people show up, how they demonstrate their teamwork and relevance. *Sell Like a Team* is a playbook for helping our great people get aligned with one another so they perform at their best and win when it counts."

—Orlando Esposito, Executive Vice President and Head of Asset
Management Group, The PNC Financial Services Group

"We operate as a global organization with employees, clients, and relationships, doing business in multiple countries. In order for us to be successful, we come together and collaborate as a team across borders and lines of business . . . which has its challenges. What Michael Dalis gives us in *Sell Like a Team* are powerful insights and valuable tools that prepare our client-facing teams to go to market together and also enable our managers to coach them so that we win when it counts."

—Jed Plafker, President and Executive Managing Director,
Franklin Templeton International

"Through decades of both research and client experience of my own, I know that enabling real team performance is a challenge. So it's not so surprising that it has taken so long to link 'team basics' to sales groups. In *Sell Like a Team*, Michael Dalis will increase your appreciation for, and show you how to overcome, the challenges of selling effectively with colleagues and partners."

—Jon Katzenbach, Managing Director, PwC, Founder, Katzenbach
Center at Strategy&, and coauthor of *The Wisdom of Teams*

"Michael is a different kind of sales coach. He has an uncanny ability to connect with sales teams. He's had a major impact on me personally. He delivers not only high-performance effective tools, but an approach that is very tangible and customized. Michael avoids the generic and addresses head-on what it takes to successfully sell in a matrixed environment with multiple stakeholders. His new book, *Sell Like a Team*, is a classic example of how the right game plan, coupled with the right preparation, elevates highly skilled, high-stakes sales teams to new levels. I strongly recommend it."

—Jeff Wagoner, Commercial Leader, US & Canada,
GE Capital Industrial Finance

"The ability to create a collaborative, successful sales team is an art form—one that Michael has distilled into parts that business leaders can readily implement with great results. *Sell Like a Team* is a must-have road map for any organization looking to master today's ever-changing, high-stakes sales environment."

—Julie M. Howard, Chairman and
Chief Executive Officer, Navigant

"This book is long overdue. Countless deals have been lost in the boardroom because sales teams don't perform as a single unit, because people don't know their roles, and because teams have not planned and prepared. *Sell Like a Team* will provide you and your team with the only philosophy and actionable framework you need to win your high-value, high-visibility dream clients. Use this book as your guide for all team sales calls."

—Anthony Iannarino, author of
The Only Sales Guide You'll Ever Need

"My research shows that organizational silos often block skilled professionals from successfully seeing and solving their clients' most important issues. In *Sell Like a Team*, Michael Dalis gives you the winning game plan for creating teams that inspire client confidence and demonstrate your firm's ability to collaborate across disciplines."

—Heidi K. Gardner, PhD, Distinguished Scholar,
Harvard Law School Center on the Legal Profession

SELL
LIKE A
TEAM

*The Blueprint for Building Teams that **Win Big** at **High-Stakes Meetings***

MICHAEL DALIS

New York Chicago San Francisco Athens London Madrid
Mexico City Milan New Delhi Singapore Sydney Toronto

1 2 3 4 5 6 7 8 9   LCR   22 21 20 19 18 17

ISBN   978-1-259-86115-4
MHID   1-259-86115-5

e-ISBN   978-1-259-86116-1
e-MHID   1-259-86116-3

McGraw-Hill Education books are available at special quantity discounts to use as premiums and sales promotions or for use in corporate training programs. To contact a representative, please e-mail us at bulksales@mheducation.com.

To Sandy, my love and my life

To Melissa, forever my baby girl

To Mom and Papa, my inspiration

To Bill, we miss you

CONTENTS

PART III
CREATING A MORE COLLABORATIVE CLIMATE IN YOUR ORGANIZATION

FOREWORD

Are you a senior executive charged with delivering aggressive revenue growth? Are you a team leader of employees with diverse areas of expertise and varying levels of skill? Are you on the front line and preparing yet again to answer the dreaded "How are you different?" question from a new prospect, when you know in your heart that the intangible rather than the tangible is what sets you apart? Are you skeptical about the notion that there is any new ground to be covered on how to improve sales results when that book has literally been written thousands of times? If your answer is yes to any of these questions, then *Sell Like a Team* is a must read.

By way of background, I have spent 25 years in the service industry and can honestly say I have attended dozens, if not hundreds of training sessions on how to sell. In most of those cases, it took me less time than the length of the training session to forget what I learned. Selling was often positioned as a game of cat and mouse. "Create the need." "Find the pain." "Don't stop at the first no." Over the years, the training sessions improved—as did their focus on the client, but most were rigid in approach and required those following the program to completely reinvent their way of doing business. I am not one who is opposed to radical change when needed, but I always believed that the most effective way to improve results was to help people incorporate repeatable principles into their current way of working. Once learned and practiced, those principles enable the person or team to more effectively identify areas of need, that when addressed, improve the lives of their clients and prospects. Said succinctly, the focus on selling must be replaced by a focus on *solving*.

As the world has become more complex, so has selling. The individual sport is now a team sport. Significant opportunities now require the participation of senior leaders, subject matter experts, and relationship managers. The margin of error for winning is razor thin and asymmetrical to the vast opportunity for losing. Teammates are often separated by time zones—sometimes by continents. Buyers are well informed and highly sophisticated. Competition is fierce. Pricing is transparent. Deadlines are tight.

If the last paragraph put a lump in your throat, it was by design. Team selling is seriously hard work. As one of my colleagues puts it: "The days of being able to 'show up and throw up' [meaning dump everything you know on prospects in hopes they will buy something] are over." Winning in today's environment takes practice. It requires strategy, it requires flawless execution, and it requires the relentless pursuit of value for all parties involved.

Those who have worked professionally with Michael, as I have many times over the years, know that he believes deeply in the importance of relevance. *Merriam-Webster Dictionary* defines the word *relevant* as "having significant and *demonstrable* bearing on the matter at hand." It is derived from an ancient Latin word, *relevare,* which means "to raise up." In the pages that follow, Michael has woven together his life experience, professional experience, and independent academic research to produce a guide for developing (raising up) teams and individuals alike. This book achieves the high standard of relevance, by having a *significant and **demonstrable*** impact on the success of team selling. Michael addresses the challenging topic of building teams with a rare combination of humor and respect. His clear intent is to honor the individuality of each team member as well as the leaders and professionals who support them. Winning is about the effectiveness of "we" rather than "me."

Not only is Michael a gifted author, but he is also a natural teacher. I have partnered with him many times over the past decade and have seen firsthand how even the most hardened veterans open themselves to a new way of doing business given the credibility, compassion, and candor that Michael brings to the craft of team selling. While the work is not easy, my teammates embraced Michael's approach because *he demonstrates a deep respect for the needs of clients.* Selling is all about structuring *relevant* solutions and truly serving clients. Beyond relevance, Michael stresses the need for authenticity. To put it bluntly, in order to achieve success, who you are and what you sell has to be real.

In *Sell Like a Team*, Michael deliberately and succinctly outlines a step-by-step process for building winning teams—or selling squads, as he calls them. The reader will learn the repeatable formula for creating, organizing, practicing, executing, and re-grouping that enables teams of all shapes and sizes to maximize their potential. Importantly, the concepts can be seamlessly integrated into your current business practices. But it will require work to win more. Yes, you must take time for a real pre-call meeting. Yes, you must leave your comfort zone to deliver and receive honest and actionable feedback. Yes, you must accept that the whole is greater than the sum of the parts, when each part is carefully selected and calibrated. And yes, you must practice.

While this book will challenge your current thinking, Michael masterfully demonstrates that each individual concept passes what I refer to as the "commonsense test." After all, who doesn't think it is a good idea to prepare for a meeting? Who would suggest that *not* listening to a client or prospect is better than listening? Therein lies the powerful and elegant simplicity of Michael's approach. He knows from experience that many, if not most, teams have the raw ingredients necessary to be successful. But without a process, without connecting the dots between the little things and the big things, without self-awareness, peer feedback, and careful preparation, even the most talented teams will fail.

As a four-year-old child, I first heard the sound of Bruce Springsteen and the E Street Band blasting from my older sister's record player. I was immediately drawn to the fullness of the sound, and for me, the music had a transcendent quality. Now, 40+ years later I remain a devoted fan and have spent more money on concert tickets than I would ever admit publicly. Why am I talking about Bruce in the foreword to a book about selling? It's simple. Anyone who has ever witnessed a Bruce Springsteen and the E Street Band show knows that Bruce and the band bring 500 percent night after night after night. Even after all the years and all the miles and all the shows, they treat every audience as a new audience. In a recent interview Bruce talked about how the band could just "feel" what every other member was going to do at any given moment. A great rock critic once wrote that the E Street Band was capable of finding and filling musical space like no other—effortlessly and completely free of conflict. Bruce and the band have committed to bringing their absolute best to every audience, every night in hopes of creating magic.

As someone who leads or supports selling teams, you may not consider yourself a rock star, but what if you could develop a sixth sense with your teammates? What if you and your teammates could seamlessly and effortlessly handle questions and overcome objections? What if you and your teammates truly treated every client and every prospect the way Bruce treats his audience? What impact would that have on your clients' success? Your organization's success? Your teammates' success? Your own?

When done right, selling is a noble profession. It is about listening, it is about thinking, and it is *all* about solving. The framework and approach outlined in *Sell Like a Team* is a statement of values and value: Trust Matters. Intentions Matter. Preparation Matters. Authenticity Matters. Relationships Matter. Honesty Matters. Delivering Value Matters. And above all else, Excellence Matters. *Sell Like a Team* will help you deliver excellence for clients regardless of which colleagues join you at a sales meeting.

Enjoy the road ahead of you, it's an important one. Happy reading.

Thomas P. Melcher
Executive Vice President
Managing Executive, Investments and Chief Investment Officer
The PNC Financial Services Group

PREFACE

A jazz quartet. A Navy SEALs unit. A TV production crew. A marching band. A Formula 1 pit crew. A football team's offense. A surgical unit.

You've probably encountered many instances of great teamwork throughout your life and may have wondered: What makes great teams great? What common characteristics do they have? How do these traits lead them to become high-achieving, successful teams, year after year?

Since you've picked up this book, I'm guessing you work on teams that sell together and you're looking for those key characteristics to make your team great—collaborative, supportive, winning.

You've come to the right place. Whether you lead or contribute to teams that collaborate to sell new business, retain and develop existing clients, or cultivate third-party partnerships, this book is for you.

In your world, you may have noticed that more and more of your pivotal new business or client meetings require multiple players working in sync. You may have also noticed that conducting a well-orchestrated group sales meeting or pitch is a rare occurrence and one that is more difficult to achieve than it appears on the surface.

That's the primary reason I decided to write this book: to give you a process for building an effective selling team and, as a result, help you win more consistently.

I realized early in my selling career that one of my differentiating talents was coaching teams that were getting ready for big pitches and pivotal client meetings. It occurred to me at some point that though this came naturally to me, it was a foreign concept to many of my peers. I realized that my ability linked back to an earlier experience in my life. Long before studying finance, getting my MBA, and embarking on a rewarding banking and investment management career, I spent my youth as an actor in New York City. This included television commercials and live theater. Remember the movie or TV show *Fame* ("I'm gonna live forever . . .")? The setting was a place called the High School of Performing

Arts, a school that trained and developed actors, dancers, and musicians from across New York City. Well, that school is real and I trained there as an actor. In addition to learning how to perform, move, and behave during an audition, my acting experience taught me how to work well as part of a team—people from diverse age groups, experiences, cultures, and ways of thinking. I developed what I like to call a "group performance discipline." In addition to understanding my role and learning my lines, I also recognized how important it was to work together with others—crew, directors, and other actors—in a way that allowed the broader company to perform effectively as a team. To stage a successful production, everyone depended on me just as much as I depended on everyone else. We practiced together; learned to trust one another; performed together; and shared feedback, failures, vision, and successes.

Fast-forward to my professional career in finance. As I began to take on responsibilities for client relationships, and later, business development responsibilities, I realized that I used the same group performance discipline I had learned during my acting days to prepare for, execute, and follow up from sales meetings. This discipline helped me win and retain business; lead many successful teams in sales pitches; and later, as a manager and consultant, coach teams and their members on how to work as a unit in order to drive more wins.

As a sales coach, I have worked across a wide variety of industries with hundreds of selling teams; several thousands of sales managers, sales professionals, account managers, and subject matter experts; and numerous senior management teams. The principles contained in this book are road-tested and current, reflecting the challenges faced by selling with others to drive revenue, and helping you to pave the path to success.

I believe that selling is a craft—and only a small percentage of people do it exceptionally well. Team-based selling is becoming more common; yet doing it effectively is even tougher than selling alone. This book's goal is to raise your awareness about the complexity of team selling and show you how to do it exceptionally well. Whether that means winning new business opportunities by pitching with several colleagues, or working with one partner to retain existing clients, you will learn a practical process and gain the tools to help you build winning selling teams, or enable their success as a coach or contributor.

INTRODUCTION

Two stories from the Olympics, two unexpectedly different outcomes . . .

In 1980 the USA men's hockey team won gold at the Olympic Games in Lake Placid, NY. All amateurs, they were known as Team USA. In the semifinals, they overcame a heavily favored Soviet Union team, which had won all but one of the prior seven Olympic competitions and boasted a roster of several world-class players. The USA team took the lead in the final period and held it to win this legendary contest. Team USA then defeated Finland in the finals to secure the gold medal. The US squad included 20 players—9 had played together at the University of Minnesota for their Olympic coach, Herb Brooks, and 4 were teammates at Boston University. (Coffey, 2005)

In contrast, let's look at the star-studded USA men's basketball team at the 2004 Olympics in Athens. Coached by Larry Brown, an NBA coach and future Hall of Famer, the team's roster included NBA MVPs Allen Iverson and Tim Duncan, and future superstars LeBron James, Carmelo Anthony, and Dwyane Wade. This was not the same team that had qualified the USA squad in 2003 for the Olympics (the Dream Team); in fact, only three members of that team remained. In the 2004 contest, Team USA lost in their first-round game. By 19 points. To Puerto Rico. Though they managed to advance to the medal round and beat Spain, which had been undefeated, they just barely made it onto the platform for a bronze model.

How does one group of highly paid superstars underperform, while a different group of amateur athletes from different schools outperform? And how can their experiences help you develop a cohesive, winning selling team?

Well, there are, of course, significant differences between selling and sports teams—all of which have nothing to do with height, vertical leap, stick-handling ability, or skating skills!

Imagine a group from your organization in its last stages of preparation for a final sales pitch. The lead salesperson is feeling confident about the team he or she is bringing; has thought through the opening comments; believes strongly in the excellence of the presentation, research, and materials; and will provide several new insights and offer provocative questions to challenge the buying committee's thinking about the project.

In this scenario, the team's CEO will also be attending and has reviewed the lead salesperson's briefings and key talking points. The CEO feels confident about conveying the organization's commitment to the client's goals.

Also participating are two subject matter experts (SMEs), who have carved out time, beyond their research and client work, to review the salesperson's briefings and the presentation materials. Based on their deep experience and knowledge, the SMEs are certain about the strength of their capabilities and their ability to communicate them to the client.

They all meet in the lobby of the client's headquarters; in some cases, they are meeting for the first time and introduce themselves. Then they confidently walk together into the client's boardroom.

Fast-forward to their departure from the meeting: the confident smiles are gone. What happened?

They weren't in sync to sell.

Once the client committee and selling team took their seats, here's what occurred:

- As the lead salesperson began to speak, so did the CEO. The salesperson yielded and the CEO spoke unexpectedly for several minutes on the strength of the organization.
- The introductions took a long time, mostly due to one of the SMEs spending several minutes describing the organization's current research focus. Already, the "team" was more than 10 minutes into its 60-minute time slot.
- The other SME, when it came time to discuss his area, nervously presented his material page-by-page—with little client engagement.
- Throughout the meeting, there was very little actual conversation with the client—even during the Q&A portion of the pitch.

- When the procurement officer did ask a question about the team's pricing proposal, the team looked at each other for a few moments before the salesperson responded. This was followed by the CEO, who provided a slightly different answer.
- At the 60-minute mark, as one of the SMEs was wrapping up her section of the presentation, two of the committee members got up from the conference table to get some lunch, which had been brought into the conference room, and the chair of the client committee thanked the team for coming.

What happened? It's what didn't happen before the meeting that really matters.

Here were representatives from an organization with the capabilities and commitment to win the business. They had pulled together professionals with credibility and experience, and who put in the time to prepare for the pitch. Yet, even with strong individual players, the group lost.

Sound familiar?

That, in a nutshell, is what this book is about—to help you avoid this scenario and instead, learn a proven process and build a cohesive team that wins. Perhaps just as importantly, you will learn how to analyze what went wrong when you don't win, so you don't make the same errors twice.

This book is not about the important work that groups do when they develop strategic account plans, and it's not about teamwork for its own sake. It is about how solid, in-sync teamwork impacts the execution of account plans and performance before, during, and after client meetings.

The book and its proven approach draws from my 30 years of experience in team selling—as a successful salesperson, account manager, leader, consultant, and sales coach.

This book leverages academic research. Though very little research has been done on selling teams, quite a lot has been conducted on the characteristics of high-performing teams and managing pressure. To illustrate the key aspects that unify winning teams, I've included both solutions and true stories from my own experiences and a wide variety of business and nonbusiness examples, such as sports, the arts, the military, community organizations, and more. These are all aspects you can begin to develop and implement on the selling teams you lead, coach, or contribute to.

As you read, you may find yourself thinking a range of different things like: "Hey we do that!" or "I should probably do that more." or "Uh, we never do that." The point is never to overwhelm you. Rather, I want to be certain that, whatever your experience and skill level today, there is something significant for you to gain by reading and using this book.

Here is how the book is organized:

Part I is about understanding and navigating today's external environment.

Before you can sell effectively with a team, it's important to understand how buyer and seller behaviors have changed since the "great recession." Recognizing the external environment as it is today will allow you to adapt and sell effectively in more complex, multiparty interactions. In this part, you will learn what "selling squads" are and what they look like across industries. Because teams that sell together typically convene for a high-stakes moment, we will also look at how pressure affects your team's work, and I will provide key insights for ensuring your team doesn't sabotage its own potential when it counts most.

The final topic in this first section is about qualifying opportunities. This subject will be familiar to experienced salespeople, yet it is important for salespeople at all experience levels to gain an appreciation for why qualifying opportunities grows in importance when working with others; and how, by collaborating, you can elevate your ability to select and pursue the right opportunities.

Part II covers how to build effective selling squads.

While Part I focuses on helping you recognize today's complex selling environment and how tough it is to sell exceedingly well with a team, Part II unpacks the proven process for choosing the right members for your group, and for helping them become a cohesive, in-sync team during the preparation for a pivotal client meeting. You will learn the process for planning your team's work efficiently and to avoid information gaps, mistakes, and last-minute heroics. You will learn how to structure an effective practice session that prepares your team to perform with excellence. And you will learn how to execute a unified meeting plan that is aligned with the interests of client stakeholders and conveys the collective strength of your team. I will also share what needs to happen after the client meeting. You'll learn to conduct an effective debrief that ensures your team is on track to deliver on client expectations set during the meeting and enables both team members and the group to grow professionally.

The process I've laid out supports the most extreme scenarios—high-stakes meetings or presentations with multiple players on each side of the table. You can apply this same approach, in a scaled-down form, to any meeting in which two or more people come together to sell to a new client or retain an existing one.

Part III covers the actions you can take today to create increased collaboration in your organization.

This part addresses the key contributors to selling squads—including senior executives and subject matter experts—and how they can maximize their positive impact on a sales meeting. I will also discuss the inevitable time-crunch: when you have minimal time to prepare, there are shortcut steps your team can take to increase your chances of winning rather than winging it. I also cover the complexity of price negotiations when others are involved, and how to stay cohesive, simple, and focused. You will learn about "selling energy" —how to get it and keep it, and how it impacts your team's (and your own) performance. Finally, I will cover the barriers that get in the way of teamwork and simple, proven steps to overcome them.

Each chapter throughout the book is structured to include common mistakes, proven research, real-life examples, time-tested solutions, and best practices that will help you lead and contribute to more effective selling squads.

A few words on how to get the most out of the time you invest in this book. Have you heard the joke about the best way to eat an elephant? One bite at a time. That visual may not work for you on many levels. As the analogy relates to reading this book, however, there is a lot here to consume. Take it one section at a time. To retain and apply what you learn along the way, you will find at the end of each chapter a work page to capture key points you'd like to remember; and questions to focus your preparation for your highest potential opportunities today. You will also find a worksheet at the end of the book to distill what you have learned into a clear, specific action plan that is ready for you to implement to sharpen your overall approach and results.

Whether you are a senior leader, sales manager, salesperson, client executive, subject matter expert, or any other contributor to selling squads, you will find road-tested tips, techniques, and tools that you can begin using immediately to drive uncommonly excellent teamwork, successful customer meetings, and winning outcomes.

Ready to dive in? Let's go!

PART I

NAVIGATING A NEW EXTERNAL ENVIRONMENT

CHAPTER 1

THE SUPER SELLER MODEL

We love superheroes and superstars in all lines of work—business, politics, sports, music, and the movies. Magazine covers, advertisements, and cereal boxes all feature the faces of CEOs, entrepreneurs, political leaders, athletes, pop artists, and movie stars, and we follow them on Facebook, Instagram, and our Twitter feeds. We hold them up as the ideal toward which all "ordinary mortals" should strive.

Does your organization have super sellers? You know, the handful of sales pros revered for their successful track record and widely recognized as the elite. Many organizations don't just focus on recognizing the talents of these super sellers, they try to replicate them. Consider how much work goes into assessing and recruiting sales talent; training them; coaching them; providing them with sales effectiveness tools; and acknowledging and rewarding them. All this focus is aimed at finding and cloning super sellers who can win business with one customer stakeholder. (See Figure 1.1.)

What if we discovered that no matter how many super sellers an organization has and how many superpowers they possess it takes more than the efforts of any one person to advance and win a significant sale in today's market? Well, that's exactly what respondents told The Richardson Company in a recent survey, "Teamwork in Selling." (Dalis, *Teamwork in Selling*, 2015, p. 3) Eighty-two percent of respondents said

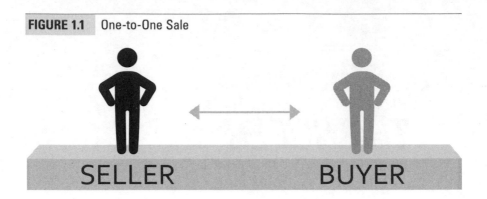

FIGURE 1.1 One-to-One Sale

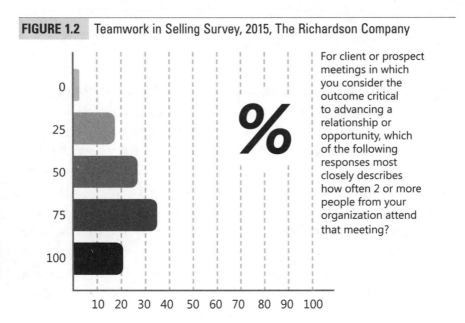

FIGURE 1.2 Teamwork in Selling Survey, 2015, The Richardson Company

For client or prospect meetings in which you consider the outcome critical to advancing a relationship or opportunity, which of the following responses most closely describes how often 2 or more people from your organization attend that meeting?

that two or more people were required for critical meetings at least 50 percent of the time. (See Figure 1.2.)

You've probably noticed in your own selling activities how much tougher it has become to close a significant sale, and how even your closest contacts have changed their behavior in the years following what's been called "The Great Recession" of 2007–2008. And you may have wondered about the increased complexity and competitiveness you're facing and asked yourself questions like:

- "Why do buyers seem more skeptical, even suspicious, of my claims and commitments?"
- "Why do my contacts seem more guarded regarding the information they are willing to share?"
- "Why are there so many more people involved in the buying decision? And why are there so many new roles as part of the process?"
- "With all these people involved, why does it seem impossible to gain access to them?"
- "Why is my client contact less able to make commitments to all but the most minor transactions?"
- "Why have purchasing decisions become so much more complicated, heavily structured, and formal?"

These are just some of the questions I hear from sales teams, regardless of company size, industry, or experience. However, before we focus on the process of building great selling squads, it's important to take a step back from your daily selling activities and consider what's driving these changes in buyer behavior. Once you understand these behaviors, you'll see that selling as a team is not the end goal; it's not an inclusive, feel-good, everyone's-a-winner exercise. Team selling is a response to these behavioral changes and is often now required for you to win.

Buyer Changes

Why are buyers skeptical? During the recession, trust was fractured between many sellers and buyers. This happened as all organizations went into survival mode and became hyperfocused on protecting their own interests. This impacted new and current agreements, operating procedures, and dispute resolutions. Partners became adversaries. Loyal customers became unpredictable. Even as the economy stabilized and buyers and sellers began to resume their mating dance, you may have noticed with your own clients that some stakeholders—particularly those responsible for vendor relationships—still harbor ill will that was created during this period. You may be waiting for time to pass and for these relationships to return to "normal." But waiting won't make it happen.

Buyers who feel as though they were burned may be waiting for you to address, rather than ignore, what happened. It is up to you to revive depleted trust levels, to eliminate skepticism and suspicion.

Acknowledging and understanding a customer's lingering concerns is the place to start. The experience and insights in this book offer proven, proactive steps. Once you have empathized with customers and better understand their trepidation, you can share ideas and actions to begin the process of rebuilding trust and relationship. And some of those ideas may include introducing your clients to more of your colleagues—colleagues you can team with to sell more effectively in order to accomplish your customer relationship goals.

Why Are Buyers More Guarded in Their Communication?

In any business transaction, information is power. As the stakes increase, so does the value of that information. Buying organizations of all sizes are formalizing their purchasing processes, and using procurement officers, consultants, requests for proposals (RFPs), and requests for information (RFIs) to reduce the risks associated with one person making a deal that impacts the broader organization. A buyer's decision to share information with you, at the expense of other sellers, can impact the terms that his or her organization is able to negotiate with you and may also damage relationships with fellow stakeholders inside his or her own organization. Imagine a scenario where you have enjoyed a close, even personal, relationship with one person in the decision-making structure for a significant purchase. In the past, she shared with you information about other stakeholders and competitors for the business. She has been at the company a long time and has managed to avoid several rounds of layoffs, but is feeling far from secure about her job, which she desperately needs. All employees now have performance goals tied to driving down operating expenses; the ability to meet these goals impacts job performance, salary adjustments, and incentives. So, she may not like you any less than in the past. Keeping her job is her priority, and she is feeling less solid than at any point in her career. Her views about helping you have changed. She now feels that giving you the type of information she has in the past may jeopardize her reputation, job, and retirement plans. And she is unwilling to risk any of those.

Why Do Buyers Seem Better Informed?

Because they usually are. According to a 2012 Corporate Executive Board study, 57 percent of buying decisions are made before your contact even reaches out to you with an initial inquiry. (Marketing Leadership Council, 2012, p. 2) (Although I have found no science to back up that exact number, what passes the logic test is that buyers have access to significantly more information today than they did 10 years ago.) In addition, stakeholders are networked internally and externally. Through internal e-mail groups, external business groups, and discussion forums such as those on LinkedIn, instant messaging, and social media platforms such as Facebook, those involved with an important purchasing decision have more access to significant information about your organization, product/service, reputation, your team, and you— even if you have never met them. Clients and potential customers are also able to leverage and synthesize information from their social and business networks to form early perceptions.

Why Is It So Tough to Gain Access to Key Stakeholders?

You may feel that access to decision makers used to be easier, and there was simplicity in that one person was making the buying decision. Because of your track record as a trusted partner and the quality company you represented, you were able to gain appointments with people when you wanted to. Consider how buying processes have affected your access over the last two decades and, more acutely, since the Great Recession. *Gatekeepers*, a term that defines those in the buying organization who block or grant access to decision makers, have increased. When you think about your clients' gatekeepers, does your mind immediately go to executive or administrative assistants who work for a senior executive? If so, consider that today, gatekeepers also include those in Figure 1.3.

FIGURE 1.3   Today's Gatekeepers

GATEKEEPER	DECISION MAKER
Procurement (purchasing) officers	Line of business leaders
Analyst	Senior staff
Consultant	All client stakeholders
COO	CEO
CEO	Board of Directors

While it may feel like a personal slight when a longtime contact no longer takes your meetings—it is important to realize that it's not personal. (Well, if your last holiday gift was a tin of nuts that triggered an allergic reaction, a trip to the ER, and massive reconstructive surgery, OK . . . it may be personal.) The move by your client's organization to control access allows it to be more efficient with its resources, protect its margins, and increase its ability to secure the vendor it wants on the best possible terms. Of course, you may still be the vendor they want, even if it feels less personal.

Who Are These Other Decision Makers?

Increasingly, purchase decisions are made in groups using formal decision processes, as illustrated in Figure 1.4. These groups can change based on opportunity and line of business, and because of reorganization and attrition. More people may become involved, roles and titles may shift around, and executive involvement may change. So your main contact at a company, with whom you have built a great relationship, is only as valuable (from a sales standpoint) as his or her influence in the decision-making group.

Procurement officers are playing a more significant role in buying decisions; where this has long been the norm for government and large corporate contracts, it has grown more prevalent regardless of company size and industry. You'll also find that private equity investors, as

---

FIGURE 1.4   One-to-Many Sale

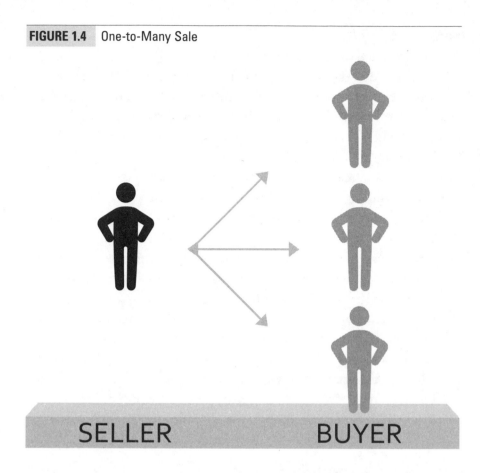

SELLER   BUYER

engaged owners, want a say on important contracts, and they are present and/or represented at more and more final pitches. Another new and influential stakeholder as of the time of this writing is the head of data security; as organizations seek to protect themselves and their customers from cyber-attacks, this role has become part of the decision-making process.

The Impact of Buyer Changes

These changes have altered how buyers buy. It's important to see your customers' behavior in the larger context of these changes.

Fewer Meetings, Higher Stakes

A meeting or call with a customer about a potential opportunity, regardless of its stage of development, may have more gravity than the stated purpose of that touchpoint. Failure to be prepared and aligned as a team may lead to an early exit from an opportunity. I remember a meeting I scheduled when I was a salesperson, with an analyst from a large hedge fund in New York City. The hedge fund was growing rapidly and I thought it was a great prospect for one of my firm's investment strategies. Due to scheduling conflicts, I was unable to recruit a portfolio manager to join me on this sales call. So, rather than give up the appointment and reschedule, I decided to go to the meeting solo, figuring it was "just an introductory meeting with an analyst." Well, midway through the sales call I found myself unable to provide in-depth answers to the analyst's many questions. He asked me about details I had no clue about. We ended the meeting cordially, and he seemed to agree that he would be open to a meeting with one of our portfolio managers in the future. He never took one of my calls again nor agreed to another meeting regardless of the firepower I was proposing to bring.

You may have already encountered more of these types of "screening meetings." They can come early in the sales process and will often determine whether or not you get to an opportunity to advance the sale.

When to Call for Reinforcements

More stakeholders on the buyer's side of the table makes it impossible for even the most super of super sellers to address their collective needs.

In order to advance the sale, you must engage others in your organization. (See Figure 1.5.) Additional colleagues include:

- Subject matter and technical experts, for their ability to engage and address the needs of additional buyer stakeholders (horizontal expansion of your selling team)
- Account relationship team, so potential buyers can assess alignment and fit with day-to-day contacts (vertical expansion of selling team)
- Senior-level executives, to demonstrate commitment and trust (*vertical* expansion of selling team)

FIGURE 1.5   Many-to-Many Sale, Networked Buyers

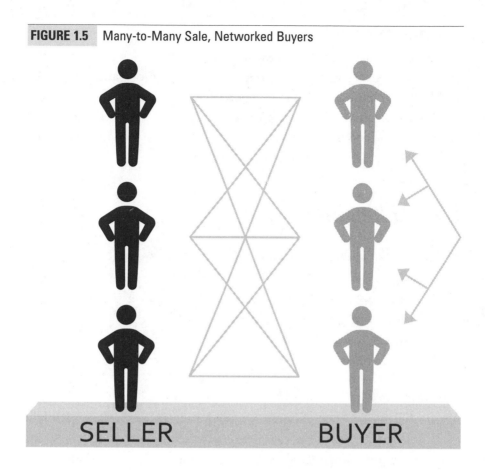

SELLER   BUYER

Increased Pricing Pressure

With buyers employing a more formal purchasing process, including RFPs; using gatekeepers to block access; and leveraging and sharing increased information, you're selling in a high-pressure storm system that can hit you hard. At times, you may feel that there really is no difference between your organization and your offer versus the buyer's other options. If the buyer is successful in making you believe this, what's the only thing left to set yourself apart? Price, of course. You feel commodified and compartmentalized—and it was all by design; even if there are substantive differences between your offer and your buyer's other options.

Opportunities Tough to Qualify

Because there are more decision makers involved and it's gotten tougher to gain access to them, generating the type of information that will enable you to qualify a deal is more challenging today. Yet, as you will see in Chapter 3, qualifying opportunities becomes more critical as you add people to the selling effort. Involving more people from your company equals greater investment and greater risk.

Seller Changes

As a salesperson, you are employed by an organization that, like buying organizations, has been hit by similar environmental changes and forces. Consider some of the changes you've seen over the past several years from within your own organization. They might include some or all of those discussed in the following sections.

Intense Revenue Pressure

Across industries, one common theme I hear from the salespeople I coach is that the market has never been more competitive. There are not only more competitors, they are more aggressive. The natural hierarchy within markets seems to have broken down. Sellers that had historically been big-game hunters are going down-market to generate more revenue. Sellers that had carved out happy niches in the midsize or smaller markets are driving upmarket to protect and grow their franchises.

Increased Franchise Leverage

Among larger selling organizations that have built out or acquired new business lines, there is more pressure to generate a return on those investments. How does this translate? Senior leadership stresses the importance of leveraging the entire organization. There is a greater focus on enterprise-wide selling (larger opportunities that span multiple lines of business) and cross-selling (customer referrals from one business area where a relationship exists to one where it may not). To convert that focus into actions, many organizations are including specific targets for cross-organization selling to salespeople and account managers.

Distributed Resources

Coming out of the Great Recession, organizations went through many forms of restructuring to peg human resources at an appropriate level for current market realities. Rather than having easy access to subject matter experts in your local office, you may now have to share SMEs with a larger region and compete with a broader audience for their time and attention. For enterprise-wide opportunities that cross multiple disciplines, you may need to pull these specialists from multiple locations, which becomes even more complicated. Depending on availability and subject matter expertise needed, the people you're able to line up for a customer meeting can change quickly. As illustrated in the Introduction, it is quite common today for people who have neither met nor worked together before to find themselves, for the first time, on the same side of the table at a sales meeting. The cost to this is the "familiarity factor" —an advantage that comes from working closely with others over time, so you are able to trust and lean into them during meetings. In addition, different people have a wide range of comfort levels, experiences, and skills with the type of meetings you will encounter.

Access to Information and Technology

Selling organizations have invested in technology and resources that make it insanely easy to access buyer and competitor information. Do you remember when Dun & Bradstreet fax reports, microfilm, and microfiche were the most innovative technological advancement? As a salesperson, you have better access, too—better intelligence on buyers and competitors than you could have imagined 15 years ago. Tools such as Wealth-X in the wealth management space exist in every vertical. They aggregate news on clients, prospects, and competitors and make it available for selling organizations' client-facing professionals. What are you doing to leverage this information?

Access to technology is changing how you deliver a pitch and how you access and share information with colleagues. To be seen as current and ahead of trend, sellers are experimenting with technology that goes beyond PowerPoint presentations. Tablets with apps such as OneNote can be used to add notes and illustrations to slides that can make your pitch more dynamic and interactive. In some organizations, pitch teams bring for each stakeholder a customized tablet, preloaded with presentation materials. Inside selling organizations, customer relationship management (CRM) systems, such as Salesforce, serve as a platform to facilitate information sharing.

The Impact of Seller Changes

These changes within selling organizations have impacted salespeople in several ways:

- **Forced collaboration**: There is increased pressure on salespeople to cross-sell. This requires super sellers from one business area to join forces with super sellers from other business areas. What could possibly go wrong?!? (You will see in Chapter 2.)
- **Pressure to close**: Though sales managers often talk about the need for larger deals (which typically take longer to close), they are under pressure to drive immediate revenue. As a result, you may feel frustrated at times by what seem like conflicting goals: invest time in bigger potential sales or hit your quarterly goals by loading up your schedule with sales calls on dubious prospects and closing smaller, quick-hit types of deals that may not lead to more significant opportunities.
- **Networked selling teams**: Buyers expect your selling team, regardless of the silos they represent in your organization, to be networked and aligned.

When buyer stakeholders accept a face-to-face meeting, they expect to learn something about your organization, your team, and your solution that they couldn't discover on their own. (See Figure 1.6.) They

FIGURE 1.6   Many-to-Many Sale, Networked Buyers and Sellers

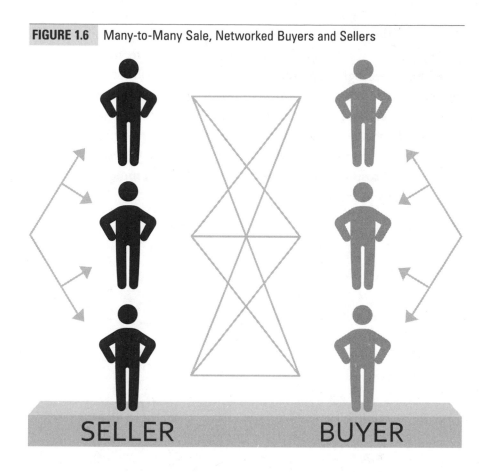

want you and your colleagues to bring new insights; thought-provoking questions; an idea based on the advance research you did. If you and your team show up with basic information and average questions, you risk falling behind to better prepared competitors.

Selling Team in Sync

Super sellers are highly effective in their individual selling skills; but it is not a given that they will be effective team leaders. Likewise, great collaborators don't automatically make for great selling squad leaders. Groups that sell together effectively operate in sync, as a unit, adopting the super seller's sales effectiveness and leveraging the collaborator's sense of teamwork. Given the wide range of sales effectiveness among individual members representing different roles, lines of business, regions, and cultures, it is no small feat to get the right people at the right meeting, and performing as a team, when it matters most.

Here's the good news: your competitors face the same pressures. You know what's even more powerful than talking about "dedicated team" in your RFP response, presentation materials, or comments? Demonstrating that you are one.

CHAPTER 1

NOTES TO SELF

1. Key points to remember:

   a. _____

   b. _____

   c. _____

2. Opportunity you are working today: _____

   _____

   a. Changes in the external environment may have impacted the client organization in the following ways:

   _____

   b. You need to: _____

   _____

3. To improve your long-term sales impact, you would like to:

   a. Stop: _____

   b. Start: _____

   c. Continue: _____

CHAPTER 2

ENTER THE SELLING SQUAD

In the mid-1990s, there was a brief flurry of academic research on the subject of selling teams. Professor Mark Moon of the University of Tennessee and Professor Gary Armstrong of the University of North Carolina, for instance, shed some light into this area and attempted to lay the groundwork for future research in their paper "Selling Teams: A Conceptual Framework and Research Agenda." (Moon & Armstrong, 1994, pp. 17–30)

Moon and Armstrong felt there needed to be a distinction between what they called "selling teams" and "selling centers." What Moon and Armstrong called "selling teams" you may recognize today as account teams, or key account teams. Account teams generally have a strategic focus and broad membership. They are populated with people who know and work with a client, across an organization's business lines and geographical footprint. Leadership and membership are often defined by managers and tends to be long-term (notwithstanding organizational and personnel changes). Account teams are strategic in that their collective work is focused around developing and executing a plan to build a specific customer relationship. The execution part of the planning can include pitches and meetings to accomplish their strategic account goals.

A different kind of team that Moon and Armstrong introduced through their work was one called "selling centers," which they defined as colleagues who come together tactically for one opportunity, only to disband afterward. They coined this name for these types of groups to align with what some researchers at the time called "buying centers"—a group of stakeholders, within a buying organization, charged with making a buying decision. (Moon & Armstrong, 1994, pp. 17–30) Today you would probably refer to them as a pursuit team, deal team, pitch team, or even selling team. I call them selling squads.

Selling squads are groups of two or more people from the same or an affiliated organization who come together to successfully gain some kind of commitment from a customer or prospect. Such commitments could include advancing or closing a new business opportunity with a prospect, or retaining, renewing a contract with, or winning new work from an existing customer. Types of meetings could include a new business pitch, a product or technology demo, an account review, a capabilities review, a due diligence meeting, and so on.

Here is where account teams and selling squads connect. When account team members successfully schedule a meeting to discuss a new opportunity, a selling squad is created. And the selling squad may include members from outside the account team who have not interacted with the customer. For example, let's say you're a member of the account team for ACME Pellets. One of the goals defined in your account team's plan is to positively shape ACME's perceptions of your organization. To achieve this goal, the team has included in its action plan for the year "arranging a meeting to begin the process of shaping perceptions." You agreed to take on this action item and proceeded to call a new stakeholder who influences buying decisions in this area. You realize this person may be unfamiliar with your firm's capabilities since this will be the first time you have sought work for this line of business. You schedule a meeting with this stakeholder and two of his colleagues. As part of your preparation for this meeting, you create a selling squad and begin recruiting members who can help you—perhaps a subject matter expert and someone to run a demo.

So, the selling squad in this case is comprised of three members—one from inside and two from outside the account team. Following this meeting, this particular trio may never work together again.

The work of both account teams and selling squads is equally important. The former is strategic and the latter is tactical. Effective account planning lays the groundwork for a selling squad to come together. In Part 2, you will learn the tactics for deploying selling squads that work together effectively and succeed in their missions.

CHAPTER 2

NOTES TO SELF

1. Key points to remember about selling squads:

   a. _____

   b. _____

   c. _____

2. Think of selling squads that you have led or contributed to.

   a. Which was most effective? Why? _____

   _____

   b. Which was least effective? Why? _____

   _____

CHAPTER 3

ALL IN OR ALL OUT

According to CSO Insights' 2015 Sales Performance Optimization survey, 21–26 percent of business that gets sent out for bids ends up with the status quo, no change. (CSO Insights, 2015, p. 7)

So, one in four deals that populate pipelines will simply drop off as a loss. Think of the time and energy that you invest pursuing a deal; an investment you can't get back. Many salespeople find this 21–26 percent range shocking. Shockingly low, that is. How often does this happen to you?

Consider the typical chain of events triggered by a request for proposal (RFP) in your own organization. The excitement is amplified when the RFP is large and from a well-known buyer. The salesperson broadcasts the opportunity through conversations, messaging, and customer relationship management (CRM) pipeline updates. Then people are taken off other work to create the proposal response—writing, editing, reviewing, approving. And this is the least expensive part of the pursuit process.

A few weeks pass, and the buyer calls with the news that you have been selected as one of three finalists. You put the phone on mute, let out a primal scream, and pump your fist wildly. Yes! He asks whether you can present to their committee. In two weeks. In Buffalo. In January. On your birthday. Your answer? Absolutely!

Here's where the investment snowballs. You begin calling in reinforcements. You will need to show executive commitment (vertical expansion of the selling team) and subject matter expertise (horizontal expansion of the selling team). Your selling partners are hesitant, but, after your heavy cajoling, pleading, and begging, they agree to change their schedules to join you in Buffalo. Excellent! Over the following two weeks, each member of this group will commit hours to review your presentation and provide you with additional materials. They will each prepare their own comments, join in on one or more group calls, and eventually travel to Buffalo to attend the customer meeting. What is the actual investment? First there are expenses for airfare, rental cars, meals, and hotel, multiplied by each member of the group. Even greater is the opportunity cost of time: for you, time available for prospecting or preparing for a key meeting with a high-potential referral source; for your senior leader, there is less time available to finalize a strategic plan that will turn around the company's declining profitability; for your subject matter expert (SME), a delay in publishing a thought leadership piece in response to a competitor blog that is gaining traction across social media channels. And, of course, there is no shortage of other needs that could be addressed by the associates who instead handle the travel arrangements; and who load, print, bind, and ship presentation materials, often changing personal plans to stay late and sprinting to the UPS office to make within moments that night's final pickup.

How do you balance investment and opportunity? The best salespeople with whom I work and coach are master qualifiers. Qualifying opportunities is consistently discussed as a best practice among leading salespeople and organizations. It's what allows sales teams to have the time to properly plan, prepare, and practice, and to win consistently.

I find that many salespeople continue to struggle with qualifying leads, even though it's a skill that has become significantly more important to have. With more stakeholders, less access, and more pressure to close profitable business, qualifying has become tougher. It can be challenging to determine the following aspects of an opportunity:

- Each stakeholder's perceptions
- How you and your organization stack up relative to competing options
- What is driving the buyer's interest in change (remember that 24 percent and the inertia of the status quo)

■ How well the buyer's budget and cost expectations line up with
your profitability guidelines

Deciding when to pursue or pass on an opportunity when you
are the only one involved is one thing; it's important, but the decision
affects only you. When you choose to involve others, the importance of
pursuing the right opportunities grows. So it is worth a quick review on
what it means to properly qualify an opportunity.

In the previous scenario—Buffalo in January—the salesperson
decided, consciously or not, to pursue the sale. What were his criteria
for making this decision? It may have been the new logo, the appeal
of a brand-new account, or the size of the potential opportunity. It is
surprisingly common for salespeople to pursue nearly every opportunity
that comes their way, without considering the actual investment.

What should be the criteria for making a solid go/no-go decision in
pursuing an opportunity, especially before ramping up the investment
by including others on a selling squad?

The Four Why's to Qualify

Qualifying is the process of assessing the "closeability" of an opportunity. To do this, I engage what I call the "four Why's to qualify." Some
of these might surprise you.

1. **Why must the customer do this?** How do the gains for the
   customer to pursue this initiative outweigh the costs and risks
   of change? These costs and risks to the buyer vary depending on
   the change. Beyond the price of your products or services, costs
   can include consultant fees to assess the solution and plan the
   implementation, staff training costs, systems development costs,
   and more. And there will also be opportunity costs as people at
   the buying organizations focus on implementing your solution,
   shifting their attention from other focus areas.

   The risks of failure could impact their operations, their
   liability, their brand, and their careers.

To overcome the perceived safety of the status quo, the selling team can play an important role in persuading key decision makers as to why the benefits of change outweigh the costs and risks. This net gain is what makes an opportunity real. An opportunity isn't real just because an RFP is issued and you are invited to a finals pitch.

2. **Why must they do this now?** What is happening in your client's organization that makes it critical to pursue this purchase this year, this quarter, or today? You know from your own company that organizations focus their attention and resources on those actions that most directly help them to overcome their major obstacles and accomplish their goals. What makes this opportunity one of those priority actions that will expedite the customer organization's progress toward a goal relative to other actions that are available? Here again, the selling team can play an important role by helping stakeholders see an alternative path or timing to what they had considered.

3. **Why must they do this with you?** How successful have you been in linking the rationale for change with your capabilities and differentiators? This may be something the selling team needs to address in its key stakeholder meetings. A winnable opportunity is one that your organization can compete for and win. Many factors go into that assessment. Beyond a solution that aligns to the buyer's needs, how strongly are you positioned with those in the decision-making structure? How is your organization perceived, given past work? Are the right people available to be part of the pitch team and/or part of the implementation team? How do your offer and your relationships stack up versus those of the competing options?

4. **Why should you do this with them?** Here's one that might surprise you. Too often, sales professionals pursue opportunities without regard to the impact on their organization or their own time. In my experience, this is usually due to production pressure. The value to your organization, beyond the revenue, may include penetration into a new market, weakening a

competitor by taking away its flagship account, or establishing a track record in a new discipline. As a selling squad's leader, you should be able to convey to your team the value of an opportunity before starting the costly process of pursuing it. Worthwhile opportunities are those that, when your client calls with the news that you won the business, you can't wait to get off the phone so you can share the news with your team and across your organization. If your reaction to that call is, rather than joy, a sense of dark clouds on the horizon rapidly moving toward you, a feeling of uncertainty about whether you will be able to deliver, that deal is not worthwhile. Winning teams have healthy discussions about whether opportunities are worthwhile, before pursuing them.

A qualified opportunity is one where there are strong reasons attached to each of the four Why's. When you check a potential deal against these four questions, you can be sure that you're investing the time because you're certain you can win it.

What if the answer to one (or more) of the four Why's leads you to conclude that the reasons for the client to make a change or the reasons for you to want the business are not there? There are two paths available to you at that point. Path A is to continue pursuing the opportunity, ignoring the signals. This is the path I see less experienced or less skilled salespeople most frequently choosing. All the signs are flashing red and the eternal optimist thinks, "So what you're saying is I've still got a chance!" On the upside, the opportunity remains in your pipeline and allows you to show sales activity. On the downside, you are taking time away from better opportunities—for both you and your selling squad members.

Path B is the road traveled by more experienced and skilled salespeople. You move on. It can be tough, especially for a deal you badly want to win. But you come to accept, with the support of your selling squad, sales manager, and/or coach, that it might be the wrong organization, the wrong stakeholder, or simply the wrong time. Disqualifying an opportunity early frees up your time to pursue more winnable deals with greater gusto.

What if the answer to one or more of the four Why's is a big fat question mark? The reasons are unclear. One of your priority actions with that opportunity should be to do more digging to convert that uncertainty into either high conviction or a more intense focus on pursuit of the opportunity or low conviction coupled with your decision to move on.

In my experience, effective selling squad leaders (like super sellers) are never frantic. They have excellent conversion rates because they are clear on why they are pursuing deals in their pipeline and they make the time to win them. Funny thing, they also have the most success in recruiting colleagues to their selling teams; people want to be part of a winning effort.

If this process of qualifying deals describes you, you are the exception in selling, rather than the rule. Many salespeople feel as if they are chronically drowning, frantic, and/or frustrated. They feel great pressure to chase every deal, and as a result, lack the time needed to prepare for those meetings that represent their best chances for success. They are, in effect, placing an equal bet on every opportunity that comes along. Their pipeline becomes big and unwieldy, their conversion rate is low, and over time they become less able to recruit colleagues to their selling squads.

Your selling squad can play a helpful role in qualifying an opportunity. Consider this: in your personal life, who do you turn to in order to help you make sound decisions? It's likely people you trust, those who can help you gain and assess information so that your decision is unbiased and offers the best outcome. While you may not have a well-established relationship with everyone on your selling squad, you do want to consider who can best help you make an objective decision that offers the best outcome to your organization, your team, and to you.

In addition to looking for strong reasons behind the four Why's to qualify, there are four best practices connected to the process of qualifying opportunities. These represent the common threads I see among effective selling squad leaders across industries:

1. Be willing to walk away from deals that lack strong responses to the four questions.

2. Engage a broad set of buyer stakeholders well before an RFP is issued to avoid the constraints that can occur once the RFP is in play and to aggressively seek information that will enable you to answer the four questions.

3. Create trust within your selling squad so that members feel comfortable sharing intelligence, interests, and viewpoints with one another, and provoke candid discussions about why an opportunity is or is not qualified. Arrive together at that decision.

4. Leverage your sales coach. Because of compensation structures and pressures to meet quota and other metrics, it is easy to lose objectivity. If you have access to a sales coach (which we will discuss in Chapter 7), he or she can help support your decision making, whether it is to double down or to fold.

The current selling environment, with less access, more stakeholders, and higher P&L pressure, make it both tougher and more important to qualify opportunities. Pursuing a deal with others is a significant investment. Leverage your access, information, team, sales leader, and sales coach (if you have one). Use the best practices outlined previously and the four Why's to qualify to ensure that the investment is a wise one.

CHAPTER 3

NOTES TO SELF

1. Key points to remember about qualifying opportunities:

   a. _____

   b. _____

   c. _____

2. Opportunity you are working today: _____

   a. Why must the customer do this? _____

   b. Why must they do this now? _____

   c. Why must they do this with you? _____

   d. Why should you do this with them? _____

3. How strong are the reasons behind your four Why's? _____
   _____

4. Will you pursue, dig deeper, or move on? What action(s) will you take next?
   _____

5. To improve your long-term sales impact, you would like to:

   a. Stop: _____

   b. Start: _____

   c. Continue: _____

PRESSURE CAN CREATE DIAMONDS . . . OR DUST

How does pressure impact your selling squad's performance?

Imagine that you sell for a technology company and that you've decided to bring Amy, a solutions architect, to an important sales meeting. Amy is confident and one of the best you have worked with; she is highly experienced and holds an advanced degree from a prestigious university. However, she has primarily focused on working with existing customers through thorny technical configurations and has had limited experience in sales meetings and presentations. In fact, Amy has never received any formal presentation training. That presents a challenge for her as demands from clients and your own organization have changed in recent years. Customer decision makers want to meet "the talent" directly so they can get a better assessment of the resources available from your company. To respond to this demand, your company is stressing the importance of including technical professionals in sales meetings. This is now a component of Amy's performance goals. So, she has been asked to participate in recent business meetings. But for some reason, Amy tends to freeze up in sales meetings and seems to generate very little client engagement. When she has asked sales reps for feedback, what she gets is general: "You did a great job; thanks for making the time."

High-pressure situations, such as a presentation or an important client meeting, tend to cause people to underperform. Group people together during a high-pressure situation, and those feelings escalate. Why?

What Is a High-Pressure Moment?

Hendrie Weisinger and J. P. Pawliw-Fry, in their book *Performing Under Pressure,* share their findings from research they have done with more than 12,000 participants over the course of a decade, drawing from their consulting work with performers in a variety of fields, such as selling teams and elite athletes. (Weisinger & Pawliw-Fry, 2015)

They assign three characteristics to a high-pressure situation:

1. The outcome is important to you.
2. The outcome is uncertain.
3. You feel you are responsible for, and are being judged on, the outcome. (Weisinger & Pawliw-Fry, 2015, p. 46)

Sound familiar?

Anyone who has pitched a project or participated in a critical meeting can agree that the outcome does matter but can be uncertain. We are also likely to feel judged by the audience we are presenting to. Adding speakers to that same presentation triggers an added level of pressure. As social creatures, we crave acceptance by our tribe. So, when we are faced with the prospect of failure, our fears of abandonment are also triggered. We fear losing the protection of the tribe if we don't perform when others are depending on us. This can happen even if you're an experienced presenter, a veteran salesperson, or the team leader for an important sales meeting. It's important to be aware that such moments will affect your behavior as well. How so?

You will recall that the first characteristic of a high-pressure moment is whether the outcome is important to you. If you're the lead, no doubt winning matters. In fact, if you're the lead, you may be only member of your selling squad whose compensation—incentive, commission, etc.

—may be directly or indirectly tied to the outcome, making it matter even more to you than to your colleagues. Duke University economics professor Daniel Ariely researched this in a study that included participants from India, MIT, and the University of Chicago, and measured the impact of success incentives on performance across several games. The researchers found that in eight out of nine of the problem-solving tasks, "higher incentives led to worse performance." (Ariely, et al., 2005, p. 19) This means the higher the incentive you or your teammates feel to perform, the more likely individual and team performance will be affected. Weisinger and Pawliw-Fry call this "an incentive trap." (Weisinger & Pawliw-Fry, 2015, p. 86) Rewards can trigger a primal need to win that award, because of a subconscious belief that your survival may depend on it. That heightened need for the incentive may lead to lying, cheating, and deception, none of which will help you align with your team or your customer.

The second characteristic of a high-pressure moment is that the outcome is uncertain. Even if the client hands you a gem like "the business is yours to lose," for most sales meetings it's impossible to argue that a win is a 100 percent certainty. Will you feel responsible for and judged by the outcome? If your answer is yes, you are likely to view the situation as a high-pressure moment. Based on my experience, most salespeople—even the most accomplished among us—feel a personal burden to perform. Or conversely, to not blow it.

What's the Impact on a Selling Squad?

So, how does pressure impact a selling squad's performance? Let's say that you've successfully recruited colleagues that are well suited to the task, and that you have created the conditions that allow this group to become an effective team (both topics that we will cover in Part II). Together, you've committed the time to prepare for the pitch and the outcome is equally important to all of you. Yet, you share a looming sense of uncertainty about the result. And the tighter the group, the greater your feelings of responsibility are likely to be to one another. As Daniel James Brown describes in *The Boys in the Boat*, the eight students who comprised the University of Washington men's rowing team and the 1936 USA Olympic men's rowing team cared for each other to such a degree that they were all willing to endure physical and mental stress well beyond their individual limits to ensure that they were not the teammate who misses a stroke that might destroy the team's success. (Brown, 2013)

In a sales meeting, the client is judging you and your unit to determine whether you're the ones who can help his or her company. To differing degrees, individual team members may feel judged by their peers. After all, the outcome of the pitch can impact your professional brand and your ability to recruit that person again for future selling squads. Your success or failure may impact the way your peers view you and the way your sales manager evaluates your performance and decides your compensation, territory, and resources.

Sales pitches and important customer meetings meet all the criteria for a high-pressure moment. The pressure is felt by each individual in the group and is heightened because others are involved. People who are charged with representing their organization in an important client meeting tend to be confident and accomplished, among that organization's best, and accustomed to dealing with pressure.

Here's how high-pressure situations impact performance:

- **Thinking becomes rigid:** Weisinger and Pawliw-Fry, in their research, found that people in high-pressure situations become "mentally rigid." (Weisinger & Pawliw-Fry, 2015, p. 66) Imagine a basketball game with two seconds on the clock and your team down by one point. You've been fouled and go to the free-throw line. You have one shot to tie the score and send the game into overtime where your team's chances to win remain alive. If you miss, your team loses. Though you have shot thousands of free throws in your life, the basket now looks like it's a mile away and the size of a thimble. Mental dexterity, or being lucid, alert, and able to adapt, is key to a successful sales meeting. Consider how tough it is to get a selling squad so coordinated that they adapt seamlessly to comments from client stakeholders and fellow colleagues in the flow of the dialogue. Now imagine a group where the members are mentally locked. They lose their ability to be creative and flexible in the moment.

- **People get defensive:** Under pressure, people usually become more defensive and less receptive to feedback. An effective team encourages a feedback loop, which allows the unit and its members to make adjustments and improve outcomes. Feedback can occur both before and during customer meetings. Before a sales meeting, the selling squad gets together to prepare and share feedback with one another. Ignoring that feedback hinders your chances of fine-tuning and strengthening your contributions for the customer meeting. During the actual meeting, stakeholders will provide feedback. If the team is unable to receive and incorporate that feedback, they blow by opportunities to course-correct in the moment.

- **Teams enter the "performance pressure paradox":** In Heidi Gardner's *Harvard Business Review* article, "Coming Through When It Matters Most," she talks about the "performance pressure paradox" she found in her research on teams within professional services firms. (Gardner, *HBR*, 2012, p. 83) In high-pressure situations, such as a client meeting, teams need to collaborate to deliver and describe a solution that feels uniquely tailored to the client. Yet, here's the paradox she discovered:

  - Teams tend to revert to what's been done before (generic, not customized).
  - Teams tend to drive toward consensus (rather than to the best outcome for the client).
  - Teams tend to yield to those on the team who hold authority in their organization (versus those who know the client best). (Gardner, *HBR*, 2012, p. 87)

Robotic, defensive, risk-avoidant. These characteristics paint a pretty grim picture of groups crumbling under the pressure of an important moment.

Yet all kinds of teams, including selling squads, successfully hold it together rather than crumble during high-pressure situations and perform close to or at their best when it counts.

Rising to the High-Pressure Moment

Think about selling squads that you have led or contributed to during a high-pressure moment. What did the team do to perform well under those conditions? As a leader, here are some actions you can take to enable your team to perform at its best during the high pressure of an important customer meeting or new business pitch:

1. **Acknowledge the pressure:** Sharing your feelings of anxiety with others puts those feelings in a place where others can help, and keeps you connected as a group.

2. **Prioritize client knowledge:** Harvard professor Heidi Gardner suggests including team members with knowledge about the client. (Gardner, *HBR*, 2012, p. 87) Be sure to give extra weight to input from team members who possess customer knowledge over those who don't; even if there are team members with greater seniority in your organization. What seems like a risky career move may be the decision that wins the business.

3. **Choose words carefully**: Weisinger and Pawliw-Fry suggest using words like "want to" over "need to." (Weisinger & Pawliw-Fry, 2015, p. 117) For example: "We need to stick to the timing we planned" unnecessarily hikes up the pressure, versus the softer "We want to stick to the timing we planned." Remember that building confidence is one of the key qualities of an effective team leader. I remember pursuing a financing deal early in my career. One day, the company's CEO strolled by my desk, told me, "the more I think about it, Michael, this deal is a must-win situation," patted my back, and then disappeared as a quickly as he appeared. Gulp.

4. **Choose an excellence mindset**: Team leaders should orient themselves around an excellence or mastery, rather than a ranking or relative, mindset. An excellent mindset means that the focus of your preparation should be geared toward being excellent—your team's best. Focusing on your performance versus a competitor creates a ranking mindset, and limits your team's

performance because it's now attached to someone else's. The relative strength of another team is beyond your control. John Wooden, Hall of Fame basketball coach, won 10 NCAA men's basketball championships at UCLA. Seven of those championships were consecutive. The roster of players rotated over that time, and it's amazing to think about how these championships were won by a different group of undergraduates each year. Here is how Coach Wooden defined success in his book *Coach Wooden's Pyramid of Success*: "Success is peace of mind that is the direct result of self-satisfaction in knowing you did your best to become the best that you are capable of becoming." (Wooden & Carty, 2005, p. 17) Instead of getting distracted by the presence and pressure of competitors, short time frames, and a changing cast of colleagues, enable team members to simply focus on being the best they are able to be as a unit. This subtle adjustment can be a powerful one.

5. **Practice together:** Yes, this means rehearsing. While you are probably not performing a concerto during your finals presentation (are you?), the principle of "practice makes perfect" still applies to a sales pitch or important customer meeting. Without practice, what's your likelihood of operating as an in-sync selling squad at go-time? Practice means many things, including testing your approach and comments with stand-ins who are willing to role-play the client, video playback, and/or coaching and extended team feedback. Rehearsing together reduces the feelings of self-consciousness that often occur when presenting in front of others for the first time. There is a big difference between writing down and thinking about the words you will say, versus saying them in front of others. That feedback flow will allow the team to refine its pitch prior to the moment it counts the most.

We will talk more about how to conduct an effective practice session in Chapter 9.

It is ironic that the pressure of an important meeting or pitch is what creates the need for people to come together as a selling squad.

Because it is this same pressure that can hurt individual performance and cause group effectiveness to fray. Carefully structuring your interactions and communications enables your team to respond to high-pressure situations, including a sales pitch or client meeting, effectively and collectively.

CHAPTER 4

NOTES TO SELF

1. Key points to remember about pressure and selling squads:

   a. _____

   b. _____

   c. _____

2. Opportunity you are working today: _____

   a. What actions could you take to enable your selling squad to perform at or near its best at the meeting or pitch?

   _____

3. To improve your long-term sales impact, you would like to:

   a. Stop: _____

   b. Start: _____

   c. Continue: _____

PART II

BUILDING SELLING SQUADS THAT WIN

CHAPTER 5

A FOUNDATION OF TRUST AND CREDIBILITY

In *The Boys in the Boat*, Daniel James Brown tells the story of a group of eight country boys at the University of Washington who came together and, despite all odds, defeated teams from elite rowing schools in the Northeast, and qualified for the 1936 Olympic Games in Berlin. This underdog team ultimately won a gold medal at those Games. The process for some of the men who were competing for the seats on that boat began four years earlier. (Brown, 2013)

Unlike sports such as basketball and hockey, in which one team is created to represent a school, large universities often create multiple crews to power several rowing "shells." At UW, there were four boats: one varsity, one junior varsity (JV), one sophomore, and one freshman. The eight seats on both the varsity and JV boats could be occupied by any undergraduate, regardless of year. Now, unless you've rowed crew at some point in your life, you might assume that since they represent the same school, the UW rowers would have tremendous comradery. Actually, these are highly competitive men who train hard, and there is typically strong competition among the different boats from the same school. The greatest competition in the UW case was for the varsity boat's eight seats.

Two years prior to the Olympics, an unusual event occurred far away from the boathouse that set the teamwork that eventually led to the UW's team National Championship win and Olympic gold medal into motion. During the summer of 1934, three UW rowers, each from a different boat, happened to find themselves working side-by-side as part of the massive construction crew building the Grand Coulee Dam. Though they had barely talked previously, they disliked each other because of their positions on different boats. However, away from campus and with grueling work to be done, they got to know each other and eventually learned to trust one another. When they returned to the UW boathouse after the summer, their coach, Al Ulbrickson, put them together in the same boat, and they developed a bond that would eventually lead their team to be the fastest eight-man boat in the world. (I will talk later about how to find, recruit, and fit together the right puzzle pieces for your selling squad.)

Think about the selling squads to which you have contributed as a leader or member. How would you rate the level of trust among those that produced a winning effort and those that didn't? Mutual trust and credibility matter as much to a selling squad as they do for an eight-person crew team with a desire to consistently win.

Let's imagine that you are a relationship manager who has assembled a meeting with colleagues to retain an important customer. The customer stakeholders have been frustrated by what they perceive to be a lack of attention and, in particular, your organization's antiquated resources relative to competitors in the market. This meeting is a make-or-break situation for your company.

You've scheduled a pre-call preparation meeting. The group gathered in the conference room includes your CEO, a technology specialist, and a salesperson from a new product area in another division. If thought bubbles were visible over the heads of each person in that room, we might see the following:

CEO: "Watch and learn, people. This is why I'm the CEO."

Technology specialist: "What a waste of time; this relationship manager can't even remember to change his password and archive his e-mails, how is he going to manage this meeting?"

Salesperson (from another division): "I can't wait to show the CEO how fantastic I am, so I can transfer to a better division."

You: "I hope I don't blow this, especially since this is my first time working closely with the CEO. I should be fine if the technology guy doesn't throw me under the bus like he did the last time we were in a meeting together."

Have you been there? Can you put real faces on each of these colleagues?

As the group looks at one another, their thoughts reflect the reality of many groups that must come together for an important meeting with a client, prospect, or partner. In this particular scenario, most of the people barely know each other; they have never worked together before and may never work together again. Selling squads can include a fascinating combination of people who are familiar and unfamiliar with each other; they may have positive, checkered, and/or negative history with one another. They can include the experienced and the inexperienced, the confident and the tentative, the skilled and the unskilled.

Roadblocks to Building Trust and Credibility

Before we talk about best practices for building trust and credibility among teammates, let's discuss the pitfalls that prevent selling squads from arriving at sales meetings as trusted colleagues:

- **Making assumptions:** You assume that everyone knows what you do, knows what they need to do, and that everyone is as committed as you are to winning the pitch. In the previous example, with you as the relationship manager, you know the customer and how to present, and it's important to you personally that you succeed in retaining the account. How important is this pitch to the other team members? How different are their perspectives and levels of commitment?
- **Not knowing each other:** When a meeting is important enough that you ask colleagues to put aside other responsibilities and commit their time, consider how infrequently people sync as a team to execute a flawless client meeting. Even with experienced presenters and intact groups that work together frequently, this is not a simple task. Consider how much tougher

the task becomes when the people in your pre-call meeting are unfamiliar and untested.

■ **Avoiding conflict:** In trying to assemble the "right" combination of people for your selling squad, you may miss or ignore cues that they are not aligned with you. As the group gets deeper into its collective work, these cues become less subtle and more overt. This might lead you to lose focus on your goal and instead spend precious time and energy on keeping the group from imploding.

■ **Lacking feedback:** This obstacle is often connected to avoiding conflict. You may have seen team leaders trying to keep things positive. Most people know they are not perfect collaborators or presenters. Glossing over or ignoring opportunities to coach people to a place where they can make stronger contributions erodes your trust, your credibility as a leader, and your chance to close the deal. Better to provide authentic feedback or coaching before the meeting (even if it means having an awkward moment between colleagues) than to have an uncomfortable or unsuccessful sales meeting.

Building Trust and Credibility

People who perform together as an effective unit are mutually credible and trusting. The credibility part means they've got what musicians call "chops," or the skills to contribute an important aspect to the group's work. If you and a colleague are part of the same organization, but have never worked together, you are each sizing up the credibility of the other. Think about how hard you work to build credibility with a stakeholder in a client relationship. Do you do the same level of work with colleagues before asking them for an introduction to one of their important clients?

Credibility is part of the foundation for effective relationships. Trust is the other part. And there is an interesting link between the two. You may know many people whom you consider to be credible or capable. And you also know people you have come to trust. For important sales meetings, think about why you would refrain from choosing colleagues who are highly adept but have proven to be undependable in the past and why you might avoid considering trusted colleagues who might lack credibility in a specific area you need. Then, consider how you gravitate to those who are both credible and trusted.

In his book, *Team of Teams*, Retired General Stanley McChrystal discusses how Navy SEALs are trained and addresses how trust plays an important role in that process. (McChrystal, 2015) It is easy to assume, based on how SEALs are portrayed in movies, that they are humans of gigantic proportions and superhero strength, speed, and skill. And to produce such superhumans, the training program must be all about building that strength and weeding out the weak. The Basic Underwater Demolition/SEAL, or BUD/S, training is a six-month program through which all candidates must pass to become a Navy SEAL. Roughly 160 candidates enter the program, more than half of whom drop within their first month. In McChrystal's words, "the purpose of BUD/S is not to produce supersoldiers. It is to build superteams. The first step of this is constructing a strong lattice of trusting relationships." (McChrystal, 2015, p. 96) This is done formally by assigning candidates to five- to eight-person boat crews on the first day, and these crews stay intact for the duration of the six-month program. This is reinforced informally by leaders who insist that people travel through their daily activities with a "swim buddy." This promotes teamwork over the solo superstar. This is done, McChrystal continues, "because teams whose members know one another deeply perform *better*." (McChrystal, 2015, p. 98)

The stakes for an important sales or client meeting, while not life-or-death as they are for SEALs, are professionally high for those involved. And mutual trust and credibility among selling squad partners—regardless of whether they are employees of your company or an affiliate —are bedrock elements of producing a winning outcome.

So what are some ways to build trust and credibility within the selling squad you have assembled?

You might find it helpful to have and to use a process for developing such partnerships. You will visit a related topic in Chapter 15 on tips

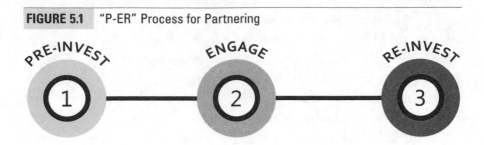

FIGURE 5.1   "P-ER" Process for Partnering

for selling with affiliates. For now, keep in mind the acronym "P-ER" (short for "partner") to represent: Pre-invest, Engage, and Re-invest. (See Figure 5.1.)

1. **Pre-invest:** This captures the actions you take prior to identifying and recruiting someone to one of your selling squads. Here are some of the ways you can pre-invest in relationships:

   ■ Invest time: With few exceptions, I have found that sales professionals tend to invest far less time developing their internal relationships than they do their external ones. Think about the way you prepare for a significant meeting with a center of influence, a key prospect or high-potential client, how you manage the discussion at each and how diligently you follow up. How does this compare with the time you put into getting to know your fellow employees in different roles, disciplines, or affiliated companies? It is tempting to assume that your colleagues—since they're paid by the same company—view the opportunity you are working on with the same level of importance you do. You may automatically assume that once you have defined their contribution in your mind, they should just do it, exactly the way you have imagined.

   As a salesperson, you know how to conduct a client-focused sales meeting. You know that the best sales meetings are those where your counterparts are so engaged that there is a lively exchange throughout. What if you prepared for and conducted your internal meetings the same way you did your external ones?

For example, you might use the following framework:

Open: to connect and frame the discussion

Ask: to better understand your colleague's aspirations, goals, challenges, etc.

Position: to propose ideas that link your interests to theirs

Close: to gain commitment and clarity on next steps

■ Start early: Trust and credibility are built in person over time. In other words, be patient. You may enjoy chatting on your phone, video calling on FaceTime and Skype, or sending out e-mails, instant messages, and texts. They are far from the best or fastest way to create tight internal partnerships. Think of trust and credibility as relationship capital; it's created when you make the time to connect personally, to understand each other's motivations and skills. Establish relationship capital throughout your organization. Leverage your travel schedule to meet people outside your region and folks in business lines you may not have supported in the past. It is much easier to begin building trust before the pressure mounts during the lead-up to an important sales or client meeting.

If initiating contact with a stranger feels uncomfortable, try adapting the following language for your personal use:

My name is Jane Janeway, and I'm responsible for business development in Amalgamated Industries' Construction division. I heard through one of my contacts that you are doing great work in a similar part of the Engineering division. I'd love to schedule a time to meet with you, get to know one another, share what we're each working on, and find ways to collaborate to create better outcomes for customers and each other. Are you game?

▪ Understand the ingredients of trusting relationships: In LaFasto and Larson's research covering more than 6,000 team leaders and members, the authors found four qualities in trusting professional relationships: (1) they are constructed with honesty and respect; (2) they are productive, leading to better outcomes; (3) there is mutual understanding; and (4) they are self-corrective, meaning through mutual understanding and honesty both parties are willing to change their behavior to produce better outcomes. (LaFasto & Larson, 2001, pp. 37–38)

2. **Engage:** Asking someone to join you on an important sales call is a big deal. We will address the topic of who to ask and how in Chapter 7. For now, keep in mind the following ways to gain mutual trust and credibility when you engage colleagues on a selling squad:

▪ Be flexible: There will be times when you will lead a selling squad and need others to play supporting roles at an effective sales meeting. Other times, you will be the one in the supporting role, while others lead. Trusting colleagues are aligned, rather than competing with one another, in their performance goals. David Breskin, in his book *We are the World*, describes how in 1985 a group of 45 leading musical stars of the day—including Bob Dylan, Michael Jackson, Bruce Springsteen, and Stevie Wonder—came together in a Los Angeles studio to produce a record and music video that raised millions of dollars for starving refugees in sub-Saharan Africa. In his invitation to the handpicked leading artists, producer Quincy Jones prominently referred to "checking your ego at the door." (Breskin, 1985, p. 19) To accomplish the mission, it was essential that each artist, accustomed to calling the shots and dominating the spotlight, be willing to play a supporting role in this case.

▪ Address (don't avoid) conflicts: Consistent with LaFasto and Larson's findings, Susan Wheelan, in *Creating Effective Teams* states that "task conflict is essential for teams to become effective and productive." (Wheelan, 2010, p. 27)

3. **Re-invest:** How many times do you leave a group sales call and miss the opportunity to grow and learn from your colleagues?

   ■ Share feedback: Whether it's before or after a meeting, be willing and prepared to exchange feedback. We will cover the process of giving and receiving feedback more in Chapter 9. Since it relates to building trust and credibility with potential and existing selling squad members, you may wish to lay the groundwork for feedback exchange early. Seek agreement as you begin working with internal partners to share feedback. If this sounds awkward, you may be missing opportunities to sharpen your selling skills. Here is an example of how you might initiate the exchange:

   > I'm always looking for feedback to get more effective in my selling activities and to boost my win rates. I would love your feedback before and after our client work together, and I would be willing to do the same for you. How would you feel about that?

I find that many colleagues and affiliates act as if the relationship-building process starts and ends at "engage," the point where someone is recruiting a selling squad for a customer or prospect meeting. Mutual trust and credibility are built over time and, often among intact teams, invisibly. In this world of pop-up teams, you may face the much tougher task of creating trusting relationships with people you may barely know within a short time frame and when the pressure is high. P-ER will remind you that the process for building such relationships begins well in advance of creating a selling squad, and continues after the conclusion of a sales meeting. Scan your internal organization, start identifying potential partners, and begin cultivating relationships with trusted and credible colleagues throughout your organization. That way, when it's time to build an effective selling squad, you'll be able to engage and then re-invest in these relationships. Remember: Pre-invest, Engage, and Re-invest (P-ER) to partner.

CHAPTER 5

NOTES TO SELF

1. Key points to remember about developing mutual trust and credibility with selling partners:

   a. _____

   b. _____

   c. _____

2. Think of three colleagues or affiliates with whom you would like to, but don't currently have, strong relationships. What actions would you be willing to take, and by when, to pre-invest or re-invest in these relationships?

   a. Partner 1: _____

   b. Partner 2: _____

   c. Partner 3: _____

3. To improve your long-term sales impact, you would like to:

   a. Stop: _____

   b. Start: _____

   c. Continue: _____

CHAPTER 6

THE BUILD PROCESS

Think back to successful team efforts in sales meetings. How were you and your colleagues able to produce that?

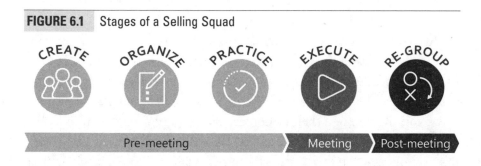

FIGURE 6.1 Stages of a Selling Squad

CREATE · ORGANIZE · PRACTICE · EXECUTE · RE-GROUP

Pre-meeting · Meeting · Post-meeting

The Build Process illustrated in Figure 6.1 most likely resembles the stages you went through. There are five stages to building an effective selling squad in the months, weeks, and days leading up to a pivotal client meeting:

Stage 1 **CREATE:** Choosing colleagues to help you win

Stage 2 **ORGANIZE:** Planning your preparation for the client pitch or meeting

Stage 3 **PRACTICE:** Investing time to rehearse together

Stage 4 **EXECUTE:** Aligning strongly with the client and as a team

Stage 5 **RE-GROUP:** Coordinating follow-up activities and feedback for growth

These five stages—Create, Organize, Practice, Execute, and Regroup—reflect what winning teams do to sell together effectively. The more intentional and consistent you are in employing this process, the more you will consistently succeed as a selling squad leader, contributor, or coach.

An effective selling squad leader must play three roles: salesperson, project manager, and facilitator. Much of Part II is devoted to unpacking each of the five stages of the Build Process and will also include best practices and tools, so that you are prepared to play each of these three important roles.

Before we go there, you want to ask how the Build Process fits in with your company's sales process. If your company has no defined sales process, allow me to define that here. A sales process tracks the life of an opportunity, from prospect research through post-sale follow-up. A strong sales process is based on interviews with top producers across a business and breaks down the life of a sale into its phases. Those phases might look something like those in Figure 6.2.

Attached to each phase would be a list of activities that generally occur at that point in the sale, and one or more signals that confirm you're ready to advance to the next phase. Companies that have completed the work to define their sales process, either by themselves or with the help of a sales consultant, align their customer relationship management (CRM) system with the phases of the process. This allows salespeople, contributors, and managers to make the sales process a living tool in their selling activities and coaching discussions, and to actively use their CRM as a tool to visualize how opportunities are progressing through the pipeline.

Now let's answer the original question: What's the connection between your organization's sales process and the selling squad Build Process?

There may be multiple points during the sales process, and even multiple times within each stage of the sales process, when you decide to enlist colleagues to advance a sale. (See Figure 6.3.) At each of these points, using the same Build Process illustrated and described above will enable you to create selling squads that are best positioned to win.

In the next chapter we'll start by looking at the Build Process, beginning with Stage 1: CREATE: Choosing the Puzzle Pieces.

FIGURE 6.2   Example of a Sales Process

PHASE

1. Identify prospect or opportunity
2. Initiate contact with prospect
3. Explore and qualify opportunity
4. Propose and present
5. Negotiate and close
6. Monitor success and new developments

PHASE

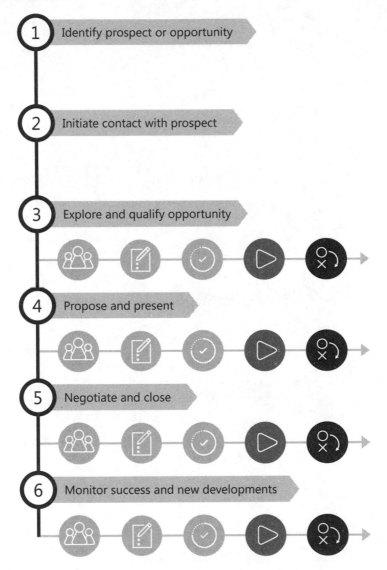

1. Identify prospect or opportunity
2. Initiate contact with prospect
3. Explore and qualify opportunity
4. Propose and present
5. Negotiate and close
6. Monitor success and new developments

CHAPTER 6

NOTES TO SELF

1. Key points to remember about the selling squad Build Process (CREATE—ORGANIZE—PRACTICE—EXECUTE—RE-GROUP):

   a. _____

   b. _____

   c. _____

2. Opportunity you are working today: _____

   _____

   In which stage (of the five) is your team today? _____

   _____

3. To improve your long-term sales impact, you would like to:

   a. Stop: _____

   b. Start: _____

   c. Continue: _____

CHAPTER 7

CREATE: CHOOSING THE PUZZLE PIECES

FIGURE 7.1 Create Stage of a Selling Squad

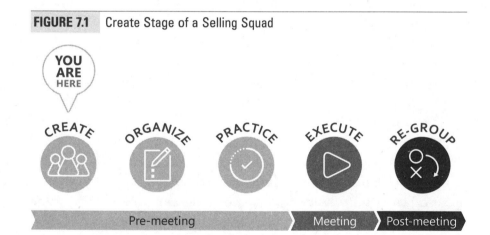

More is always better, right?

Earlier, you were introduced to the University of Washington men's crew team. Coach Al Ulbrickson faced a classic leadership challenge: who should be on the boat? Each fall, more than 100 able-bodied undergraduates show up at the boathouse for tryouts. One of his first challenges was to push those students to their limits and find the best candidates for the university on the varsity, JV, sophomore, and freshman boats.

His next challenge was to find the right mix of eight men for each of the boats. Using size and strength as the criteria misses the X factor: the magic that happens in high-performing teams that allows them to produce a result that is greater than the sum of the parts. In rowing, the synchronicity that makes it seem as though the boat is flying over the water is called "swing." (Brown, 2013, p. 275) In the years prior to the Olympic Games in Berlin, the coach made countless adjustments in the lineups for all four boats. He knew he had created the perfect combination when the eight men in the varsity boat began to beat the competition with a stroke rate that seemed much lower in contrast to the physical exertion of the rowers. They appeared to be rowing effortlessly.

As part of their reward for winning the national championships, they were given the opportunity to represent America at the games. As part of the Olympic competition, there were two rounds—a preliminary round and a medal round. After the preliminary round, the fastest boats from the preliminary round competed for gold in the next, medal round.

During the preliminaries, the Japanese boat quickly took the lead and rowed at a feverish 50 strokes-per-minute pace at its peak, splashing water everywhere. Team USA remained composed and found its swing at a much lower stroke rate in the low 30s, which allowed the Americans to methodically close the gap and seal the victory.

How did they do it? Every position in the boat certainly required a significant element of physical strength, endurance, mental fortitude, and excellence, but all elite rowers are strong and capable. This team of men learned to trust and care about one another so much that they would rather endure physical stress beyond their individual limits than let their team down. They were so deeply focused on one another as a collective unit that they were able to propel that wooden rowing shell as if it was a well-synchronized machine.

Think about those times that you were part of a selling squad that found its "swing." How did that happen? It most likely wasn't the four people who met for the first time in the parking lot, then, after some quick handshakes, walked into the customer's office. Grouping together the most effective combination of people, rather than purely the strongest individuals, so that they can find their swing in high-stakes sales meetings is the fundamental challenge in creating selling squads.

Think back to a time when you were notified by a customer that your proposal was successful and you were invited to present to the committee as a finalist. You were elated. Think about the process you went through to decide who should join you at the pitch. You mentally scrolled through and chose from your database of trusted and credible colleagues who could potentially help you win this deal. You selected each person for a reason, for the contribution you hoped they would make to a winning effort. How much thought did you give to what they would be like to work with on this pitch, or how they would mesh with the others you asked?

Early in my sales career, I was asked to join a major pitch to a large university that had selected our organization as a finalist in a multi-service provider search. Our firm was at that time highly focused on cross-selling. So the lead salesperson dutifully matched the client's various interests, as outlined in the request for proposal, with people from the firm that could address those needs, for a two-hour pitch. I was to represent one aspect of our capabilities. Members of our group were all arriving from different places for the pitch, so we were asked to meet in the hotel lobby at 7:30 that morning. It turned out that there were 12 of us, many of whom had never met before. And because of our numbers, the lead salesperson had arranged for a minibus to transport us from the hotel to the building where the presentation was to be held. Getting settled in the conference room was no easy task. There were six decision makers representing the university. Given the numbers and size of the conference room table, some of us were seated around the table but some had to take chairs against the wall. In the end, a few of us talked for about 60 seconds in the moments before the lead person wrapped up. In reality, two or three people from our group did the majority of the talking. We failed to win the business.

Based on what we've covered so far in this book, what went wrong? The opportunity was not fully qualified, and the salesperson glommed together 12 random people among whom there were varying degrees of established trust and credibility. For each of the 12 members of this group who committed to this presentation, there were substantial investments in preparation and travel time, in addition to the hard dollar cost of lodging and transporting each person to and from the pitch. You can imagine how that decision might have been made. "Gee, we don't have much time and I don't want to miss something. Better to be safe than sorry."

What would have been a better approach?

It took Coach Al Ulbrickson at the University of Washington three years to assemble the winning formula for his eight-man varsity boat. And nearly a year for that crew to come together as a unit to find its swing. What would have been a better approach for the university pitch above?

Two fundamental questions face selling squad leaders after they've scored a vital meeting with a potential client: Who? and How many people should I bring? These decisions are often made with far too little thought. Conducting an effective and successful sales meeting is tough, even for a super seller who is 100 percent effective in a one-on-one meeting. What happens to sales effectiveness when the super seller adds senior managers, salespeople from other disciplines, subject matter experts, and technical experts—each of whom may be less than 100 percent sales-effective? And even if all meeting participants are at the extreme 100 percent effective, are you guaranteed that the collective unit will perform effectively? Without synchronicity or swing in your eight-man boat or on your selling squad, there is no magic and winning is an unlikely outcome.

Roles

Jon Katzenbach and Douglas Smith, former McKinsey partners and coauthors of both *The Wisdom of Teams* (1993) and *The Discipline of Teams* (2001), point out that high-performing teams are not "limitless groups of helpful people." (Katzenbach & Smith, 2001, p. 96) They break down membership into four categories: core group, sponsor, ad hoc, and formal. (Katzenbach & Smith, 2001, pp. 94–95) For selling squads, I break this into three categories:

- **Core group:** These are the people who will be presenting at the sales meeting. This group includes those members essential for a successful meeting.

- **Extended group:** This combines what Katzenbach and Smith call "ad hoc" and "formal" members. These are colleagues who contribute unique inputs to the group planning, practice, and follow-up efforts, but whose presence at the client meeting is not required. These people are the enablers who ensure that the core group accomplishes their mission at the pitch. Examples could include a product specialist who joins one of your prep sessions to share several industry and competitive insights or an associate who has committed to play an important role in pulling together presentation materials, coordinating technology, and lining up travel arrangements.
- **Coach:** This is someone who is able to contribute direction and feedback as needed by the team. This person should be available, objective, and skilled at coaching. He or she may be internal to your organization, such as a sales manager or practice leader. A sales coach can also be external—a professional like me, for example, whom your organization retains to support you or your selling team in your interactions before and after an important sales meeting or pitch.

How do you decide who should be on the core team and who should be on the extended team?

Core = critical to having a successful meeting
Extended = enables others to have a successful meeting

Once you have established the membership of your selling squad's core group, it's important to think through and define the role each member will play within that group. If roles are left undefined, people will sort themselves into the roles they seek or with which they are most comfortable; neither of which may suit your objectives as the leader of this unit.

So what roles, beyond the leader, need to be defined for a significant client, prospect, or partner meeting?

- **Specialists:** These team members bring deeper knowledge, beyond what the leader knows, to a client conversation.

Choosing the specialist with the right experience and expertise will be an important factor in establishing credibility with your client. The specialist role can be played by subject matter experts (SMEs), business heads, or sales specialists in a specific area of capability. If they focus solely on their respective subject area, specialists risk coming across as arrogant and generic, and detract from your selling squad's efforts. But, when properly prepared and aligned with the team, specialists can play a big part in helping your team win the business. (Chapter 13 has more on how to best leverage an SME in a sales meeting.)

- **Technicians:** These professionals have deep technical knowledge in a very narrow subject area, i.e., IT, systems specialists. The role you may want them to play in a customer meeting is to address your system's ability to link with the customer's or comply with certain protocols. Technicians can play an important part in forging connections with those stakeholders most focused on evaluating technical qualifications. The risk in bringing a technician is that either the question the person was brought to answer never comes up (projecting an image of inefficiency and overstaffing in your organization) or the person falls too far down the rabbit hole when addressing the question, taking valuable time and attention away from more relevant areas. Prepared properly, technicians can increase your firm's credibility in a specific area and help the prospective client to check boxes in your favor on important questions that would not have been addressed otherwise by team members or in a follow-up discussion.

- **Seniors:** This executive is responsible for a business line or practice area, or may steer the overall organization as a partner or C-level executive. You hope this person will convey gravitas and client commitment. Your decision to include this person may be based on what you discovered about the seniority of client stakeholders attending the meeting, or what you feel needs to be conveyed in your team's comments. Without clarity on their role in this group, seniors can take over as de facto leaders of your selling squad, both in preparation sessions and in the actual customer meeting. In doing so, they can take you away from an otherwise winning game plan. If passive, they can detract from your selling efforts by looking like an overpaid figurehead. Senior-level executives, positioned properly, can play a significant role in a winning selling squad effort and may allow your team to make great strides in differentiating your organization and value proposition. (Chapter 12 has an in-depth discussion on how to make the most of including a senior manager in a sales meeting.)

- **Juniors:** This may be an analyst or internal salesperson on your team who you feel would benefit from the experience of attending an external client meeting. Juniors can also play an important role on-site at the customer meeting. For example, they could help you stay focused on client introductions and your opening comments by setting up the technology for a demo or presentation slides; they might also be able to assist you by taking primary responsibility for recording notes and coordinating any follow-up. Failing to clarify their role on the selling team could risk an improvised moment during a stressful juncture in the meeting, or their presence may simply distract the buyer.

We will talk more about how to calibrate your core group with the right size and mix later in this chapter. For now, just take note that as you build out your selling squad, each member should have a clear role on the team. And although there is no requirement that you must always include a specialist, technician, senior, and junior, attaching a role to each team member will help you determine and describe your expectations for each person.

We've yet to define one role that's key to the team's success and which may be of particular interest to you. And that's the role of the selling squad leader.

The Leader Role

High-performing teams have a leader. This section explores the qualities of effective team leadership for a team going into an important customer meeting. In following chapters, we will discuss activities on preparation, execution, and follow-up. Here, we will focus solely on qualities.

The leader of a selling squad establishes overall direction and purpose and facilitates discussion before, during, and after the meeting. For new business meetings, this role is typically played by a salesperson; for existing customer meetings, the leader may be the account manager.

Seniority in the organization is not essential; client knowledge combined with credibility and trust among her teammates are. On winning teams, this person is effective at generating ideas and discussion before the customer meeting, and skilled at managing the conversation during it. Harvard professor and expert on team dynamics Richard Hackman frames it this way in *Leading Teams*: "Those who create teams . . . have two quite different but equally important responsibilities: to make sure that the team has the best structure that can be provided, and to help members move into that structure." (Hackman, 2002, p. 130)

I did some work with a salesperson from a large consulting firm that was getting organized for a big pitch, or what consultants call "orals." This opportunity was connected to a project being done for a different division of a company that had been a client of this firm for many years. Firm leadership really wanted the work and was thrilled when its request for proposal response led to an invitation to present at orals. As in many professional services firms, the members of this group were a sharp bunch—recognized for their expertise not just within this firm but in the industries they serve. The salesperson was charged with organizing this group. He had a good track record of sales results but lacked the advanced degrees and technical experience that his group members brought. So how did he take on the leadership role? Because this opportunity had been green-lighted using the four Why's to qualify covered in Chapter 3, he was able to prioritize this opportunity over others in his pipeline. This clarity also gave him confidence to spend extra time preparing for this role. I later learned that he dominated the decisions necessary to develop and coordinate the team's work and discussions. During the pitch, everyone made the key points he had scripted for them, and everyone strictly followed the agenda the leader developed.

The salesperson was notified a few days following orals that his team had lost the business. Per the firm's standard practice, they sent someone separate from the orals team to meet with one of the client stakeholders to get feedback on the presentation and their decision. In their internal debrief, the selling squad realized that there had not been much reaction or interaction from the client contacts during the meeting. Here's what the client said in their feedback:

> Your team had by far the most experience of any of the firms we were considering and, in fact, was the front runner going into the meeting. Your presentation was solid and everyone was impressed with how well prepared everyone was. At times, however, members of your team came across as arrogant and didn't seem to interact as a team. Some of their comments were not connected to the things we are struggling with. And the business development person seemed to block his colleagues from going off script. In the end, your firm lost the business because, though you were qualified and well prepared, our buying team felt your firm would be rigid in its rules and tough to work with versus other options we were considering.

That feedback was shocking to some on the team. The team leader felt confused by this feedback. In our discussions afterward, he realized that, while he was better organized for this meeting than any other he had led, his increased focus on organization and details disconnected him from some of his teammates and what was actually happening during the client meeting.

He is not generally a command-and-control personality type, but he took on that persona during the team's interactions. He came across as inflexible to his colleagues, and this pervaded how the team came across to the client. In conversations with individual group members afterward, some felt disengaged and that their ideas were not welcomed on how to make the presentation even better. That is one extreme—the command-and-control leader.

The other extreme is lack of leadership. If we took the same firm, same opportunity, and same group and made one change—exchanging the domineering leader for a weak one—you can imagine how that might have played out. The loudest voice might have won and brought the group down a different but equally fruitless path.

So what are the qualities of an effective leader of a selling squad? The most common responses I get when I pose this question to groups are: strong, charismatic, and resolute.

According to Susan Wheelan, author of *Creating Effective Teams*, "social scientists reject the notion of inborn traits" and, further, that a charismatic leader may actually "inhibit group progress and reduce member participation." (Wheelan, 2010, pp. 77, 79) So if traits are not predictive, let's look instead at behaviors. Frank LaFasto and Carl Larson, in their work covering 6,000 team members and leaders, offer an interesting view. They asked both work group members and leaders to define what they thought were the qualities of an effective leader. Leveraging this research, here are six best practices associated with effective selling squad leaders (LaFasto & Larson, pp. 98–149):

1. **Focus on the goal:** You must be able to communicate the collective goal so that it's clear, meaningful, and current. If your team is preparing to go into an important meeting with an unhappy existing client, the goal may seem apparent—to retain the client. A collective goal is like a mantra, it inspires you and your team members. Think more broadly about the reasons that make retaining this client so important right now. What would success mean to us? Why is this critical to the firm? What are the implications if we are unsuccessful? Your performance goal might sound something like this:

   > Our goal is to hold on to this client for three reasons: (1) They are influential industry experts. (2) We want to position our company for a significant opportunity next year. (3) We want to shut down Competitive Industries' efforts to take our turf.

   Aligning strong, accomplished people in a group that may have never worked together before can be a steep challenge for selling squad leaders. As an effective leader, you should be able to keep the team members on task, despite many distractions, by inspiring them to stay focused on an important performance goal.

2. **Create a collaborative climate:** Organizational behavior researchers use word like *open* and *supportive* to describe leaders that drive collaboration. Create a space where information can flow freely and safely among individual members. Facilitate the production and communication of ideas in a way that surpasses what any one of the members could achieve on their own. Strive for equal contributions during core team discussions. In "The New Science of Building Great Teams," MIT's Dr. Alex "Sandy" Pentland discusses this notion of "equal talk time." (Pentland, 2012, p. 68) This notion can be a powerful one in enabling selling squad leaders to talk less, facilitate more, and seek equal contributions from all members. Pentland employs a "big data" approach to assessing team communication patterns, collecting data on how often and for how long team members are communicating with one another, using electronic badges. (Pentland, 2012) Figure 7.2 shows the communications patterns for one geographically dispersed work team at the beginning and end of a week during the observation. The group's members were shown updated maps daily that allowed them to grow more aware of and fix their communication biases. When you think about the selling squads you have led or contributed to, which of the pictures in Figure 7.2 would most resemble the communication pattern among members?

3. **Build confidence:** Communicate results in a way that is both fair and factual, and acknowledges member contributions. For complex, multidisciplinary, enterprise-wide new business pitches, there are countless things to be planned, practiced, developed, delivered, measured, and executed upon. In such instances, call attention to the progress that has been made, rather than endlessly focusing on what still needs to be done. This helps core and extended group members build momentum and stay on a winning course.

4. **Demonstrate sufficient technical know-how:** As a selling squad leader you don't need to know everything, but you must

FIGURE 7.2   Mapping Communication Improvement

Our data show that far-flung and mixed-language teams often struggle to gel. Distance plays a role: Electronic communication doesn't create the same energy and engagement that face-to-face communication does. Cultural norms play a role too. Visual feedback on communication patterns can help.

For one week we gathered data on a team composed of Japanese and Americans that were brainstorming a new design together in Japan. Each day the team was shown maps of its communication patterns and given simple guidance about what makes good communication (active but equal participation).

Day 1: The two Japanese team members (bottom and lower left) are not engaged, and a team within a team seems to have formed around the member at the top right.

Day 7: The team has improved remarkably. Not only are the Japanese members contributing more to energy and engagement (with the one at the bottom becoming a high-energy, highly engaged team member) but some of the Day 1 "dominators" (on the lower right, for example) have distributed their energy better.

(Source: A. Pentland, April 2012)

have enough knowledge to be a credible member of the team, who can understand how and when to best leverage the team's talents. How is your credibility with your fellow team members? Do you consider your role in customer meetings to be limited to bringing the pitch books, making opening introductions, and thanking the customer at the meeting's close? Think about what skill and knowledge you bring to your selling squad in a winning effort. It might be your customer knowledge, your track record at delivering for the customer, or your skill at coordinating the team's efforts. It's important to recognize that you need your fellow team members, just as much as your team needs you, to win.

5. **Set priorities:** As your team moves deeper and deeper into its preparation for a critical client meeting, keep the team laser focused on the goal (#1 above). As time passes and new information emerges, facilitate discussions that may restack the team's priorities, so you can all reach your collective end goal.

6. **Manage performance:** In the context of a sales or client meeting, you may very well have no reporting authority over any of the team's members. So how can you manage performance without a manager's typical toolkit of performance evaluations, compensation, incentives, and promotions? Consider embracing and recognizing the contributions that bring the group closer to attaining its goal. Acknowledging individual contributions by team members and, where appropriate, informing their managers of how well their employees are doing, can be huge motivators.

What would your colleagues say about the qualities you bring to your leadership role? LaFasto and Larson assess the effectiveness of a team leader by surveying team members on each of the six criteria above. (LaFasto & Larson, 2001) (See Figure 7.3.)

Leverage the six best practices above to drive focus, collaboration, confidence, credibility, progress, and performance as the leader of your selling squads.

You've identified potential members of your selling squad, and are focused on how to lead the team effectively. Now, let's begin to build your team.

FIGURE 7.3   The Collaborative Team Leader (Team Version)

I. Focus on the Goal

TRUE	MORE TRUE THAN FALSE	MORE FALSE THAN TRUE	FALSE	
☐	☐	☐	☐	1. Our team leader clearly defines our goal.
☐	☐	☐	☐	2. Our team leader articulates our goal in such a way as to inspire commitment.
☐	☐	☐	☐	3. Our team leader avoids compromising the team's objective with political issues.
☐	☐	☐	☐	4. Our team leader helps individual team members align their roles and with the team goal.
☐	☐	☐	☐	5. Our team leader reinforces the goal in fresh and exciting ways.
☐	☐	☐	☐	6. If it's necessary to adjust the team's goal, our team leader makes sure we understand why.

II. Ensure and Collaborative Climate

☐	☐	☐	☐	7. Our team leader creates a safe climate for team members to openly and supportively discuss any issue related to the team's success.
☐	☐	☐	☐	8. Our team leader communicates openly and honestly.
☐	☐	☐	☐	9. There are no issues that our team leader is uncomfortable discussing with the team.
☐	☐	☐	☐	10. There are no chronic problems within our team that we are unable to resolve.
☐	☐	☐	☐	11. Our team leader does not tolerate a noncollaborative style by team members.
☐	☐	☐	☐	12. Our team leader acknowledges and rewards the behaviors that contribute to an open and supportive team climate
☐	☐	☐	☐	13. Our team leader creates a work environment that promotes productive problem solving.
☐	☐	☐	☐	14. Our team leader does not allow organization structure, systems, and processes to interfere with the achievement of our team's goal.

FIGURE 7.3   The Collaborative Team Leader (Team Version), *continued*

TRUE	MORE TRUE THAN FALSE	MORE FALSE THAN TRUE	FALSE	
☐	☐	☐	☐	15. Our team leader manages his/her personal control needs.
☐	☐	☐	☐	16. Our team leader does not allow his/her ego to get in the way.

III. Build Confidence

TRUE	MORE TRUE THAN FALSE	MORE FALSE THAN TRUE	FALSE	
☐	☐	☐	☐	17. Our team leader ensures that our team achieves results.
☐	☐	☐	☐	18. Our team leader helps strengthen the self-confidence of team members.
☐	☐	☐	☐	19. Our team leader makes sure team members are clear about critical issues and important facts.
☐	☐	☐	☐	20. Our team leader exhibits trust by giving us meaningful levels of responsibility.
☐	☐	☐	☐	21. Our team leader is fair and impartial toward all team members.
☐	☐	☐	☐	22. Our team leader is an optimistic person who focuses on opportunities.
☐	☐	☐	☐	23. Our team leader looks for and acknowledges contributions by team members.

IV. Demonstrate Sufficient Technical Know-How

TRUE	MORE TRUE THAN FALSE	MORE FALSE THAN TRUE	FALSE	
☐	☐	☐	☐	24. Our team leader understands the technical issues we must face in achieving our goal.
☐	☐	☐	☐	25. Our team leader has had sufficient experience with the technical aspects of our team's goal.
☐	☐	☐	☐	26. Our team leader is open to technical advice from team members who are more knowledgeable.
☐	☐	☐	☐	27. Our team leader is capable of helping the team analyze complex issues related to our goals.
☐	☐	☐	☐	28. Our team leader is seen as credible and knowledgeable by people outside our team.

FIGURE 7.3   The Collaborative Team Leader (Team Version), *continued*

V. Set Priorities

TRUE	MORE TRUE THAN FALSE	MORE FALSE THAN TRUE	FALSE	
☐	☐	☐	☐	29. Our team leader keeps our team focused on a manageable set of priorities that will lead to the accomplishment of our goal.
☐	☐	☐	☐	30. Our team leader and the members of our team agree on the top priorities for achieving our goal.
☐	☐	☐	☐	31. Our team leader communicates and reinforces a focus on priorities.
☐	☐	☐	☐	32. Our team leader does not dilute our team's effort with too many priorities.
☐	☐	☐	☐	33. If it's necessary to change priorities our team leader helps us understand why.

VI. Manage Performance

☐	☐	☐	☐	34. Our team leader makes performance expectations clear.
☐	☐	☐	☐	35. Our team leader encourages the team to agree on a set of values and guides our performance.
☐	☐	☐	☐	36. Our team leader ensures that rewards and incentives are aligned with achieving our team's goal.
☐	☐	☐	☐	37. Our team leader assesses the collaborative skills of team members as well as the results they achieve.
☐	☐	☐	☐	38. Our team leader gives useful, developmental feedback to team members.
☐	☐	☐	☐	39. Our team leader is willing to confront and resolve issues associated with inadequate performance by team members.
☐	☐	☐	☐	40. Our team leader recognizes and rewards superior performance.

FIGURE 7.3   The Collaborative Team Leader (Team Version), *continued*

41. What are the strengths of the team leader?

_____

_____

_____

_____

42. What one or two changes are most likely to improve the effectiveness of the team leader?

_____

_____

_____

_____

(Source: LaFasto, Frank, and Carl Larson, *When Teams Work Best*, 2001, pp. 151–152)

How Many

Earlier in this chapter, you may recall that I recounted the story of a 12-person pitch to a large university for the management and administration of their endowment assets. The challenge the salesperson in that story faced is one that you may have encountered: How do you strike the right balance between being selective and inclusive? Remember that membership in your core group is selective; they are the people who must be at the customer meeting for you to win. Your extended team can be inclusive. Anybody who is able and willing to support and guide the core team is welcome to play an important role.

Katzenbach and Smith explain that a core group should contain a small number of members, "with complementary skills, who are equally committed to a common purpose, common goals, and a commonly agreed upon working approach, to all of which team members will hold each other mutually accountable." (Katzenbach & Smith, 1993, p. 96)

Losing Free Riders

There have been many studies on the optimal size of work groups, though none specifically for a selling team. Many organizational behavior specialists refer to "The Ringelmann" effect to decide group size. Max Ringelmann was a French agricultural engineer in the early 1900s whose research was aimed at maximizing team productivity and minimizing what economists often refer to as "social loafing" or as the "free rider" problem. Rather than increasing with each addition to a team, productivity increases slightly at first, but ultimately decreases as members of the larger and larger group allow others to shoulder the work. When my daughter, Melissa, was young, I coached her basketball team. She was a talented, focused, and very competitive young athlete, and would often carry the team. The more the other girls realized how Melissa could take over the game and lead them to victory, the more they allowed her to take control. At one point, it became a team of one with multiple free riders. Wheelan put it best: "successful teams contain the smallest number of members to accomplish goals and tasks." (Wheelan, 2010, p. 47)

Less Is More

Sometimes more can produce less, and less can produce more. A selling squad's core team should include only those members who will play a material role and whose presence is required to accomplish the team's goals—whether that is to win the business, to secure another meeting, or to successfully renew an agreement. Effective selling squad leaders are aware that each person added to the core team changes the unit's chemistry and can make the collective tougher to manage. Remember stacking blocks as a child? You and your siblings or friends would take turns adding a block creating a bigger and bigger tower until it finally collapsed and crashed down. My housemates and I, during our junior year as undergraduates, played a similar game with dirty dishes in the sink. Whether we're talking about stacking blocks, dirty dishes, or selling squads, the principle is the same. Think carefully about the impact of each addition when you assemble your selling squad—will they strengthen the group or cause it to crumble?

Also, consider what messages the size of your group conveys to customers. Large groups can give the impression of low confidence, limited knowledge per person, bloated fee schedules, and confusing contact points. And outnumbering customer stakeholders can be intimidating to the client, which works against the type of free-flowing dialogue you know reflects an effective sales meeting. On the complete opposite end of the spectrum, showing up alone to a meeting with multiple buyers gives off the impression of overconfidence, and conveys that the person has little influence with his or her colleagues, that this business venture is a low priority, and that your company lacks the means to obtain needed resources.

Do the Math

Between those two extremes, how many people should attend your sales meeting? Let's look at it from another angle. Think about how much time has been allotted by the customer to your team for this meeting. We can use a simple example of a 60-minute meeting or presentation, with three client stakeholders attending. If we assume that to be successful the client should be talking at least 50 percent of the time, that leaves your team with 30 minutes of talking time to allocate. This includes not only items on the agenda, but also time needed to respond to customer questions.

If you're a math geek, you might want to play with the following formula:

$N = 0.5 \times T/P$

Where:

N = number of team members
T = total time slot for pitch, meeting, or call
P = amount of talk time per selling squad member

I feel compelled to say that I developed this formula based on my experience building and coaching selling squads. This formula has only been validated by me as a sales geek and coach. I've found that doing the math helps teams focus their attention on answering "how many" before "who," and to start their discussion with a solid benchmark. Starting with the "who" question can burn a lot of time on unnecessary back and forth about who did or didn't do what at this or that sales pitch.

If you assume P = 15 minutes/person, the formula can be simplified to:

$N = 0.033 \times T$

Road testing this formula with a 60-minute meeting (T = 60), N = 0.033 × 60 = 2. Changing P from 15 to 10 minutes per person would change the factor in the simplified formula from 0.033 to 0.05 and change your answer from two people to N = 0.05 × 60, or 3 people. In terms of the visuals, this matches up nicely with the three customer stakeholders.

Remember that 12-person university pitch I participated in and mentioned earlier? Let's do the math on that two-hour presentation. So breaking down 60 minutes of talk time for our team, shared by 12 people, leaves five minutes per person. Hardly enough time for anyone to make a meaningful contribution. The formula above suggests four to six selling squad members.

How would the math have worked out for your last selling team meeting?

In meetings where the customer group is larger, things get trickier. Effective sales meetings are those in which stakeholders are engaged. And, if they are engaged, that means they are talking. The more talk time they use, the less you and your team will have. That means even fewer members, and a tougher call on who goes as part of the core team and who stays behind.

Who Goes?

So far in this chapter, we've covered the components of a selling squad (core, extended, coach) in an effective work group. We've also talked about the different potential roles within your core group (leader, specialist, technician, senior, junior), and the implications of group size. This still leaves open the question of exactly whom you should include on your selling squad. (See Figure 7.4.)

Many salespeople, once they have successfully scheduled an important meeting, begin pulling in bodies for the effort. Out of habit or routine, can you think of times you turned to some or all of the following?

- **A-listers:** Colleagues and partners who have a reputation for being big hitters and client friendly. They are frequently asked to participate in big meetings and have been connected to blockbuster wins.
- **Big guns:** Senior leaders, including those from the C-suite (to show "senior management commitment") and celebrity thought leaders to bring some star power to the event.
- **I-dotters and T-crossers:** Specialists to answer every possible question that stakeholders may ask. You know, just in case.
- **Friend zone:** People you like.
- **The swarm:** The shock-and-awe strategy, showing all—literally all—of your resources.

FIGURE 7.4   Planner 1: Purpose & People

PLANNER 1
PURPOSE & PEOPLE

Our meeting objectives:

CORE TEAM MEMBERS

| Role: | Role: | Role: | Role: |

EXTENDED TEAM MEMBERS

| Role: | Role: | Role: |

You may also have fallen into the common trap of passing over someone with a quieter personality who, despite not commanding attention the way an A-lister or big gun might, could have made significant contributions to your extended or core group.

Just like military maneuvers call for situational awareness, the same is true in building the membership in your team. There is no single approach that works in every instance, and, truly, there is merit in each of the above approaches. Being successful, senior, smart, or likeable doesn't necessarily make someone right for you as the leader, for your team as a whole, for your customer, and for this particular opportunity or meeting.

Sometimes your partners are predetermined by your organization, but often this is your call.

For your next sales meeting with multiple stakeholders, what if you paused before immediately turning to an A-lister or big gun? High-impact selling squads, as you have come to appreciate, are not random groups of smart people who magically show up at go-time and shine. They are thoughtfully constructed teams that work to get in sync so that they can sell. If you are aiming to put together a selling squad that finds its swing at an all-important customer meeting or pitch, what qualities would you seek in colleagues that will collaborate not just during, but before and after, an important sales meeting? Consider looking for the following qualities when determining who you should ask to join your selling squad:

1. **Interpersonal skills:** This goes beyond whether someone can put together and speak in complete sentences. In their research of 6,000 workplace team members and leaders, LaFasto and Larson found that effective team members were not only technically competent. They exhibit four qualities: openness, supportiveness, an action orientation, and positive personal style. (LaFasto & Larson, 2001, pp. 9–25) Viewed another way, each person you add will contribute to or take away from your efforts to win the business. Beyond their smarts, what will it be like for you and the other group members to work with them in the lead up to and the execution of an effective client meeting?

2. **Complementary skills:** Author and Harvard professor Hackman conducted decades-long research on high-performing small groups in business and nonbusiness settings. He found that among the biggest mistakes in selecting team members was little to no attention paid to diversity. (Hackman, 2002, pp. 123–125) Homogeneous groups can be fun and get through meetings quickly because there are no conflicting ideas. It's that same expediency that can create huge gaps in the team's work. Diversity of thought, including a devil's advocate, can feel inefficient at times. However, it's the inevitable push and pull that can call out missed opportunities and unleash the sort of creativity that transcends what each member could produce individually. So consider what each candidate for your group would bring to the collective effort that's different in terms of skills, knowledge, and experience.

3. **Client-specific expertise:** When a buyer invites you to present, it is safe to assume they feel your organization has the general qualifications to perform the work. Client-specific expertise refers to someone's knowledge about a client. Heidi Gardner, in a Harvard Business, reported her findings from a multiyear study of 78 audit and consulting teams in two separate professional services firms. She distinguishes between "general professional expertise" (subject matter knowledge) and domain-specific expertise (knowledge about a specific organization or client). (Gardner, *HBR*, p. 80) When faced with performance pressure, such as in a high-stakes meeting or pitch, she found that groups tend to favor the input of those with general subject matter knowledge (the tried and true) over those with customer knowledge. But it is customer knowledge that allows a team to customize the design of solutions and how they are presented in a high-stakes meeting.

   Have you ever seen leaders exclude from a selling squad people with exceptional client knowledge and a willingness to participate? I have. It can be done for reasons of ego, convenience, or to keep the group like-minded. And I cannot remember a time when such a decision produced anything other than a loss. The more client knowledge to be leveraged by your team before and during the pitch, the better.

4. **Collective intelligence:** Groups operate as a unit with a level of intelligence. This collective intelligence can be measured and used to predict success. The more experts you add, the better . . . right? According to work published by Dr. Anita Woolley of Carnegie Mellon University, and several co-authors, in *Science* in 2010, the intelligence scores of individuals were not significantly correlated with the group's collective intelligence. What was? Among the factors: social sensitivity of group members and (sorry, fellas) the proportion of females. (Woolley, et al, 2010, pp. 686–688) Think about how potential group members who bring strong social intelligence (i.e., insight, empathy, etc.) will benefit your team's decision making, both in its preparation and during a pivotal client meeting.

Figure 7.5 is an Effective Member Checklist used by researcher Wheelan. It will help you assess how well team members will assist with coordinating and facilitating group efforts, how frequently they will volunteer to take on tasks, and how willing they will be to bring full engagement to team interactions.

In my experience, the most effective selling teams are able to see each other— despite organizational hierarchy, siloes, or roles—as peers, or teammates, for the purposes of a meeting or pitch. Organizational reporting lines may feel significant to you and your team members since you are employees of that company. Reporting lines, however, have little use to clients. They are most likely seeking help to solve a problem that will help them accomplish their own goals. They are trying to see whether your organization is the one to do that. The pitch is your opportunity to demonstrate this. How your team interacts with the client and with one another conveys more than your words will. The process for being able to demonstrate this in front of a client begins far before the meeting. Set a standard for equal partnership among team members, and seek to address quickly any team member expectations for preferential status.

FIGURE 7.5 Effective Member Checklist

Please read the statements below. Circle the number that most accurately describes your response to the statement. Use the following key to respond to each statement.

1 DISAGREE STRONGLY	2 DISAGREE TO SOME EXTENT	3 AGREE TO SOME EXTENT	4 AGREE STRONGLY

Section I

1. I avoid blaming others for group problems.

    1   2   3   4

2. I assume that every group member is trying to do a good job.

    1   2   3   4

3. I treat people as individuals and don't make assumptions about them based on my preconceived notions about people like them.

    1   2   3   4

4. I do not get bogged down in interpersonal issues or personality conflicts.

    1   2   3   4

SECTION I SCORE: _____

Section II

5. I encourage the process of goal, role, and task clarification.

    1   2   3   4

6. I encourage the use of effective problem-solving and decision-making procedures.

    1   2   3   4

7. I encourage the group to outline, in advance, the strategies that will be used to solve problems and make decisions.

    1   2   3   4

8. I work to ensure that decisions and solutions are implemented and evaluated.

    1   2   3   4

FIGURE 7.5   Effective Member Checklist, *continued*

1 DISAGREE STRONGLY	2 DISAGREE TO SOME EXTENT	3 AGREE TO SOME EXTENT	4 AGREE STRONGLY

9. I encourage norms that support productivity, innovation, and freedom of expression.

    1   **2**   **3**   **4**

10. I encourage the use of effective conflict management strategies.

    1   **2**   **3**   **4**

11. I support the division of labor necessary to accomplish goals.

                                        SECTION II SCORE: _____

Section III

12. I work to ensure that the input and feedback of every member are heard.

    1   **2**   **3**   **4**

13. I work to ensure that we all have a chance to demonstrate our competence and skills in the group.

    1   **2**   **3**   **4**

14. I discourage any group tendency to adopt excessive or unnecessary norms.

    1   **2**   **3**   **4**

15. I am, and encourage others to be, cooperative.

    1   **2**   **3**   **4**

16. In conflict situations, I communicate my views clearly and explicitly.

    1   **2**   **3**   **4**

17. I respond cooperatively to others who are behaving competitively.

    1   **2**   **3**   **4**

                                        SECTION III SCORE: _____

FIGURE 7.5 Effective Member Checklist, *continued*

1 DISAGREE STRONGLY	2 DISAGREE TO SOME EXTENT	3 AGREE TO SOME EXTENT	4 AGREE STRONGLY

Section IV

23. I have negotiated, or would be willing to negotiate, with other groups and individuals to help my group obtain needed resources.

    1   2   3   4

24. I share information and impressions I have about other parts of the organization with the group.

    1   2   3   4

25. I encourage the group not to overwhelm itself with too much external information or dements.

    1   2   3   4

26. I talk positively about my group to outsiders.

    1   2   3   4

27. I keep other members of the organization informed about what my group is doing.

    1   2   3   4

SECTION V SCORE: _____

Section VI

28. When members stray off the task, I diplomatically try to bring the discussion back to the task.

    1   2   3   4

29. I go along with norms that promote group effectiveness and productivity.

    1   2   3   4

30. I encourage high performance standards.

    1   2   3   4

31. I expect the group to be successful and productive.

    1   2   3   4

FIGURE 7.5 Effective Member Checklist, *continued*

1 DISAGREE STRONGLY	2 DISAGREE TO SOME EXTENT	3 AGREE TO SOME EXTENT	4 AGREE STRONGLY

32. I encourage innovative ideas.

      1   **2**   **3**   **4**

33. I use what I have learned about group development and productivity to help my group become effective.

      1   **2**   **3**   **4**

34. I encourage the group to frequently assess and alter its functioning, if necessary.

      1   **2**   **3**   **4**

35. I volunteer to perform tasks that need to be done.

      1   **2**   **3**   **4**

SECTION VI SCORE: _____

Total Minimum Score: 35

Total Maximum Score: 140

My Score: _____

FIGURE 7.5 Effective Member Checklist, *continued*

What Is Your Overall Membership Quotient?

TOTAL SCORE	YOUR MEMBERSHIP GRADE
126+	A
112-125	B
98-111	C

What Are Your Section Scores?

Section I: Attitudes and Feelings

TOTAL SCORE	YOUR GRADE
14+	A
12-13	B
10-11	C

Section II: Processes and Procedures

TOTAL SCORE	YOUR GRADE
25+	A
22-24	B
20-21	C

Section III: Communication and Participation

TOTAL SCORE	YOUR GRADE
22+	A
19-21	B
16-18	C

FIGURE 7.5   Effective Member Checklist, *continued*

Section IV: Support and Encouragement

TOTAL SCORE	YOUR GRADE
18+	A
16-17	B
14-15	C

Section V: Intergroup Relations

TOTAL SCORE	YOUR GRADE
18+	A
16-17	B
14-15	C

Section VI: Work and Productivity

TOTAL SCORE	YOUR GRADE
29+	A
25-28	B
22-24	C

(Source: Wheelan, Susan, A., *Creating Effective Teams,* 3rd ed., 2010, pp. 71–76)

Recruiting

Sometimes the most valuable teammates need to be convinced to join your cause. And that can feel frustrating, especially when time is short and a big sale is on the line.

It is easy to fall into the trap of making one or more of the following assumptions about potential members of your selling team as you begin the recruiting process:

- They care about winning the deal as much as you do.
- They see things exactly as you do.
- They like you and trust you.
- They should sign on since you're all part of the same company.
- They see a return on their investment (ROI) in working with you on this pitch or meeting.

As with any assumption, the facts may be quite different. A potential candidate may be hampered by time constraints, competing priorities, and perhaps even their own lack of confidence in their sales or presentation skills. Much as they might like to help, they may feel their time is better spent in other areas, especially given the time it takes to prepare for and travel to and from a customer meeting. If past work together has yielded no positive results, it is possible they see little, or even a negative, return in investing time in your selling effort.

Successfully persuading prospects and clients to take action requires a solid selling process and skills. The same process and skills can also be leveraged in recruiting colleagues to your selling team. Here are some reminders and best practices:

1. **Know where you stand:** Before asking for anything, it serves you to know where you stand with your colleague and deal with facts, not assumptions. Remember that the foundation of an effective team selling is mutual trust and credibility. If you're not sure where you stand with a potential candidate, find out. Because even if the answer is no on this pitch, you may want to take actions that lay the groundwork for a yes on future ones.

2. **Convey the mission:** This connects back to the performance mission, goal, or mantra that you use to inspire your selling squad. Link your task to the work you have done to qualify this opportunity. Understanding what makes this opportunity real, winnable, and worthwhile to pursue will put conviction behind your recruiting pitch.

3. **Connect to their ROI:** In what way will their participation help accomplish their own objectives? As mentioned earlier, investing time and investing early in these relationships helps you understand how your sales opportunity aligns with their own goals.

4. **Ask:** Just as any effective sales meeting ends in an ask, in your recruiting pitch you need to ask for their participation if you want it. Remember you are not looking for people who will only show up at go-time, pull the cord on their back, and play a canned recording. The commitment you are seeking is to the mission and to become part of a group that, through its work together, will become an effective team for a critical customer meeting. How comfortable are you seeking such a commitment? Here is an example of what that might sound like:

> As you may know, we are meeting with ACME Pellets in three weeks to retain their business. There is even more on the line, with a significant enterprise-wide sales opportunity coming up next year, and Competitive Industries trying to break into our space. Your participation on the team for this meeting will convey ACME's importance to our company and position us as a solid partner both for the existing business and the future opportunity. So that you can make an informed decision before joining us, this team is investing time in preparing together to demonstrate during the meeting the teamwork our company is known for. Will you join us?

> Take the time to sort through, practice, and even get feedback on how you will ask.

5. **Go live:** It's way easier for someone to say no to a text, e-mail, or voice mail. In addition, think of how insignificant your request seems when it's made with a few keystrokes or words on a recording. If it's feasible, go see them and ask them to join you. If that's not possible, schedule phone time, so that you can review the opportunity fully.

In a perfect world, people in your own organization should make themselves available to you whenever you need them. As a salesperson who has likely encountered rejection at least once in your life, you probably have come to realize that the world is imperfect. You've qualified this opportunity. You've given thought to the size of your team, and who the best candidates for each role could be. Take the steps above, find your conviction, and deliver your most compelling recruiting pitch so that you can put together a selling squad that wins the work.

As a reminder, Figure 7.6 is the tool to leverage during the Create stage of the selling squad Build Process.

FIGURE 7.6   Create Tools

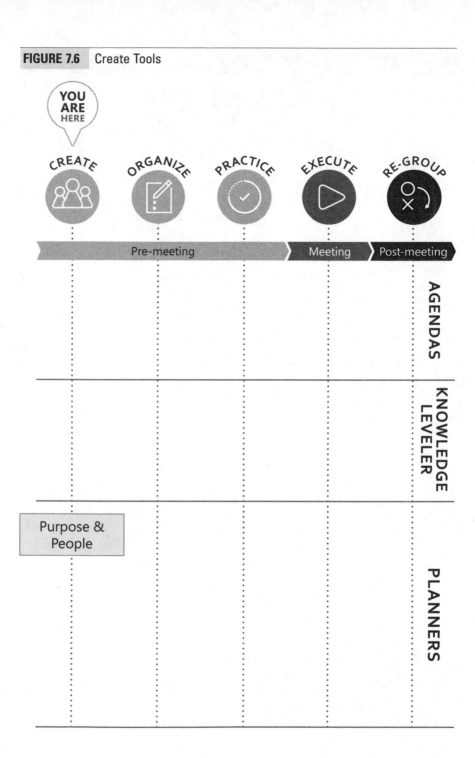

CHAPTER 7

NOTES TO SELF

1. Key points to remember about the Create stage of the selling squad Build Process:

   a. _____

   b. _____

   c. _____

2. For a team selling opportunity you are working today:

   a. How many people should be on your selling squad? _____

   b. Who will be members of the core team:

      i. Leader: _____

      ii. Senior: _____

      iii. Subject matter expert: _____

      iv. Technical specialist: _____

      v. Junior: _____

   c. Who could be on the extended team, and in what roles?

      _____

   d. If a sales coach would help you win, who could play that role?

      _____

   e. How and when will you recruit these team members?

      _____

3. To improve your long-term sales impact, you would like to:

   a. Stop: _____

   b. Start: _____

   c. Continue: _____

CHAPTER 8

ORGANIZE: PLANNING YOUR WORK TOGETHER

FIGURE 8.1   Organize Stage of a Selling Squad

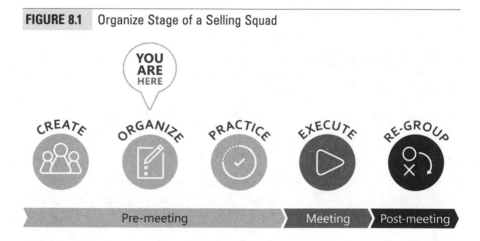

Much research has been done over the last few decades about so-called "high-performing teams" in the workplace. One broad conclusion is that the word *team* is vastly overused in business. Putting together a high-performing team is a rare feat and takes time, even under the best of conditions.

The group of colleagues you have selected to join you for a client meeting may be a combination of the familiar and unfamiliar; internal colleagues and external partners; and skilled and unproven presenters.

And while this meeting may be the most important entry on your calendar this month, your colleagues' priorities may be quite different. Achieving a successful outcome requires you to turn this group into an effective selling squad, most likely in a short time frame and under high-stakes conditions. What could possibly go wrong?

The biggest mistake I see at this stage is lack of awareness around how complex the task is. Can you see the thought bubble floating over the head of an overly confident super seller? "It's like me, but even bigger and better."

Trying to stage such a transformation in a few weeks or days, when only a handful of intact work groups accomplish this over the long term, might be unrealistic. However, we can leverage lessons from the research on high-performing teams to raise awareness and build an understanding of what makes an effective unit.

Creating the Conditions for a Well-Organized Team

Here are some best practices on how to create the conditions that best allow the people you have recruited to work together effectively as a team:

1. **Refine the group's mission:** You may recall from earlier chapters that your ability to convey the team's mission, or mantra, is one of the marks of an effective leader. A mission is about more than winning the business or retaining a client. To inspire others to keep contributing, it's important for you to define, and for the team to refine, what winning means for your organization and for the members individually.
2. **Set performance goals:** High-performing teams have clear, challenging, outcome-based goals and use these common goals to stay unified. In final presentations, the performance goal may seem clear: to win the business. How about all those other key meetings that lead up to the ultimate pitch? Here are two examples of what a group performance goal looks like:

- To move the customer from a neutral position to one where they express positive feedback on our value proposition, so that we can schedule another meeting to advance the discussion toward a new relationship.
- To gain the customer's agreement to not cut us out of the business, provided we are able to rebuild their faith in us and that we can get things right within 90 days.

Setting easy goals don't inspire engagement. Crafting goals that are realistic but stretch people's imagination has a motivational effect.

3. **Identify challenges:** There are no shortages of challenges leading up to a sales meeting. We could be lagging competitors on information, relationships, time, product, resources, capacity, and so on. By developing an honest and complete inventory of these challenges, you at least give yourself and your team the opportunity in your work together to try to close these gaps.

The word *honest* is intentionally used above. Have you ever been part of an organization or work group where people were strongly encouraged to always be positive? Being both positive and honest are not mutually exclusive. False positivity, however, as in "the Emperor without his clothes," sets your team up for failure with a game plan that's built on a faulty set of facts.

4. **Clarify individual and collective work product:** In advance of a sales meeting, there are numerous tasks that need to be completed. Some of these are best performed individually by team members; examples include developing an introduction and key messages during a capabilities discussion. Other tasks could be tackled by the group collectively. These might include the pitch book and meeting agenda. For whatever the group decides to approach as collective work product, ground rules must be established for both development and decision making.

These can include, for example, who in the group will lead the effort to develop presentation materials, what criteria will be used to decide what goes in and what stays out, and who has decision rights in case of disagreements.

5. **Define accountabilities:** As part of clarifying individual and collective work product, teams must also nail down accountabilities by task, owners, and time frames. This is about looking one another in the eye and making mutual commitments because the group understands that it will succeed or fail together.

   There are countless tools, including Basecamp, that allow multiple people to manage, monitor, and communicate about projects.

6. **Plan for conflict:** Bringing together accomplished people can produce unpredictable results. At best, a group can produce greatness and perform like a symphony, transcending the performance of any one person. At its worst, group efforts can produce disasters. Imagine, for instance, a tankful of piranhas in a fight to the death, where each member competes against the others. If as an effective team leader you are successful in generating a fairly equal distribution of talk time among teammates, there will be no shortage of opinions.

   With all voices heard, there will be conflict. The mistake most teams make is to seek consensus, avoiding conflict. High-performing teams, in contrast, are willing to fully understand differing opinions and give decision-rights to those who—because of their skills, experience, and interest—are in the best position to make a choice that helps the group accomplish its mission and goals, even if not everyone agrees with those decisions. Authors Jon Katzenbach and Douglas Smith call this "enlightened" rather than "unenlightened" disagreement. This means that even if you disagree with another team member's position, you should at the very least understand their point of view. (Katzenbach & Smith, 2001, p. 114)

7. **Sort through your communication plan:** This should include agreeing on frequency, duration, format, and roles during team touchpoints. Technology such as e-mail groups and instant messenger apps can be great to help teams separated by geography and time zones connect before a group sales meeting.

8. **Seek an objective feedback loop:** To enable your team to make course corrections en route to your goal, be sure to seek and be

open to feedback from people both within and outside your core group. Those closest to the opportunity and presentation may miss new information and changes in the buying process that are obvious to the extended group, less vocal members on your team, or your sales coach.

Enabling Feedback

Earlier, I talked about how to set up the expectation for a feedback exchange with a colleague. So, let's briefly add to the topic here by discussing what feedback is and isn't. Feedback can provoke stressful feelings in many people. "Can I give you some feedback?" Unless that question is being posed to you by a trusted, supportive colleague, you are most likely preparing to be attacked. Unfortunately, many people equate feedback with judgmental, unfair criticism because that's the only "feedback" they have received.

What is "constructive" feedback? It's information that when, accepted without filters, can help a person and team leverage strengths and address weaknesses. This assumes that the giver is trusted, and skilled at capturing and delivering information that is intended to help the receiver. It also assumes that the receiver is able to lower his or her defensive barriers to accept this information.

We will cover more fully in Chapter 18 a process for developmental coaching. But because feedback loops are such an important part of effective teamwork, it's important to mention some tips here.

Constructive feedback is balanced, specific, and honest. (See Figure 8.2.)

Balanced means there is always one or more strengths, and one or more areas for improvement. No plan, idea, or comment is either pure perfection or utter rubbish. Figure 8.3 shows a balance sheet of feedback.

Specific entails paying attention and taking notes so that you can offer advice about something that can be changed. An example of specific feedback would be: "What's awesome is the way our game plan anticipated this new development in the client's decision-making process." Whereas, nonspecific feedback would simply be "That's awesome."

FIGURE 8.2 Key Components in Sharing Feedback

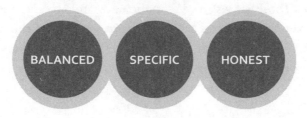

BALANCED   SPECIFIC   HONEST

FIGURE 8.3 Balance Sheet of Feedback

STRENGTHS	AREAS FOR IMPROVEMENT

Honest refers to being direct. While some might shut out brutal honesty, excessive politeness that sugarcoats a helpful coaching tip with frosting and a cherry on top is equally ineffective at delivering the point. Find the happy medium: be candid with your comments, yet compassionate with the recipient's feelings.

Receiving feedback can feel as uncomfortable as giving it. What seems to soften the blow is the notion of understanding and not judging what's being shared. Consider asking questions to clarify and taking notes. You decide what, if anything, to incorporate.

Creating a feedback loop is essential for an effective team. This can include opening a channel through which information can flow from a coach or extended team member to the core team, or simply among team members. Feedback enables your team to adapt and improve its game plan, and allows individual team members to strengthen their contributions.

Once you have decided to pursue a qualified opportunity, and *created* your selling squad by identifying and recruiting the right players to play significant roles to help you win it, it's time to *organize* your work together.

One of the investment bankers I coach shared with me a story about a past experience where she and two of her colleagues were asked to present to the CFO of a large, publicly traded company. Her colleagues were a managing director, the group's leader, and a trader, a subject matter expert. Because this trio worked together before on a similar transaction, they set up a quick phone call to prepare. They reviewed the deal and defined roles, sorting out that the managing director would lead the meeting and explain the bank's approach to structuring the transaction. The trader would address how the client would be protected from a large change in interest rates. And the banker role would to develop their pitch book and include content on the bank's experience in structuring similar trades and illustrations on how the transaction would work. The managing director reviewed logistics and travel arrangements and promised to send background information on the company. They clicked off the call. Mission accomplished. Or was it?

They arrived on time, feeling confident. As the meeting got underway, the CFO seemed to like the proposed structure, with one exception: how the bank had proposed to deal with interest rate protection. The CFO felt the protection was not worth the cost and quickly dismissed this idea. The trader jumped in and argued his belief that what they proposed was the right way to do it, and reviewed the cost-benefit analysis. According to the banker, the meeting rapidly spiraled from a conversation to a verbal battle.

Their pitch failed to win the business. When the CFO returned the managing director's call, the reason she gave was: "You didn't seem to get what we were trying to accomplish."

The group in this scenario had worked together in a similar transaction before, and rather than treating the new opportunity uniquely, they assumed it would be the same and chose to go into autopilot, simply substituting different names and numbers into a previous model that had worked for a different client in the past.

Author and Harvard professor Richard Hackman offers a number of gems that team leaders and contributors should keep in mind during the period before a pivotal meeting, including: "Mindless reliance on habitual routines results in suboptimal performance for many organizational work teams." (Hackman, 2002, p. 163)

A group of colleagues who represent their organization at an important meeting tend to be smart, experienced, articulate people who know each other and their organization's capabilities very well. And it's that very experience, or familiarity, that triggers a "mindless routine."

To transform a small group of professionals—sometimes from multiple disciplines, locations, and cultures—into a high-performing team in the short time frame between the client's call and the meeting is no cakewalk. Groups that work together for far longer may never reach that goal. So after the CFO's call, it's important to start the process with an appreciation for the work involved to move your small group of smart and trusted compadres into an effective team. As we have discussed, this will not happen on its own.

According to Hackman, "the leader's main task . . . is to get a team established on a good trajectory and then to make small adjustments along the way to help team members succeed. No leader can *make* a team perform well. But all leaders can create conditions that increase the *likelihood* that it will." (Hackman, 2002, p. ix)

Common Pitfalls

Working together as a selling squad begins at your very first planning meeting, which I call an Organize meeting. Before we talk about how to conduct an effective Organize meeting, let's look at some common mistakes you may recognize that pitch teams make at the start of their collective journey to an important meeting or pitch:

- **Assume that an Organize meeting is unnecessary:** Most commonly made by people who work together often, and especially those who work in the same location.
- **Assume that an Organize meeting can be done by phone:** Audio- or videoconference is increasingly the only option in organizations that centralize shared resources, such as practice leaders and specialists, and decentralize others such as client-facing associates. For global opportunities, the direct and indirect costs of bringing people together physically would be

impossible to justify. Those exceptions aside, groups that could easily get together still do not. And they miss opportunities to gel as a team.

- **Dump information:** There is oftentimes an imbalance in customer knowledge among the selling team. One person in the group may have been cultivating the opportunity for some time and knows the most about the client situation. To correct the imbalance, there is often a knowledge transfer, which is a one-way flow of all information gained. Dumping information, without thought to how it is organized and relevant to the team, creates disengagement and is unlikely to serve as the handoff of knowledge that you intended.

- **Accept core team absences:** This includes both people who fail to show and those who are physically present yet visibly disengaged. If core group members are missing in body or spirit during your launch meeting, this may be a leading indicator of what their contributions are likely to be over the course of your work together. How will you get them up to speed on key information, the game plan, and their role? How will they begin meshing with other team members? If you've done sales calls with busy C-level executives (CEO, CFO, CIO, etc.), you've experienced how tough it can be for them to commit time to prepare. You've also seen, then, what can happen when they join the group farther downstream— taking over, overhauling the game plan, rapid-fire decisions, and more. Last-minute engagement by even the most collaborative senior executive or team member can throw your team off what would have been a winning path.

- **Make this your only collective preparation session:** Amazingly, many groups use this first meeting as their only meeting. The discussion is centered mostly on logistics and presentation materials for the client meeting. But, as you probably know or are about to discover, an effective sales pitch involves more than a group of bodies and presentation books.

So what does an effective selling squad Organize meeting look like? Let's start with the basics.

Who Should Be There?

Ideally, your Organize meeting—or audio- or videoconference if needed—includes all core and extended group members. Especially for members who have responsibilities other than this customer situation, it is important to begin the process of grounding and aligning the people in what will hopefully become the team. Make your launch a mandatory meeting. The rule applies the same to a C-level executive as it does to a busy operations professional, each of whom committed to the pitch. No need to become a dictator or to lose your job over it, but the "mandatory" component of the launch meeting is as important in substance as it is in the message conveyed to your colleagues about the importance and complexity of the task ahead. Advance planning, using online calendar tools, and leveraging your relationships with the administrators who support your team members, will strengthen your ability to coordinate full attendance of your core team at the launch meeting.

When Should You Convene?

The easy answer is: the sooner the better. Even though there may be large gaps in what you know in the early stages, it allows you to begin creating a team vibe. How much time you have to work with will, of course, be driven by the client and situation. There is much planning to be done, and the sooner you can begin the more likely it is that you can avoid the heroics, stress, and mistakes that come with last-minute preparation.

What Should You Cover?

There are three broad areas that should be covered during all team touchpoints: knowledge leveling, planning, and practice. (See Figure 8.4.)

"Knowledge leveling" is the process of making certain that all members of at least the core team are bringing each other current on

FIGURE 8.4   Organize Goals

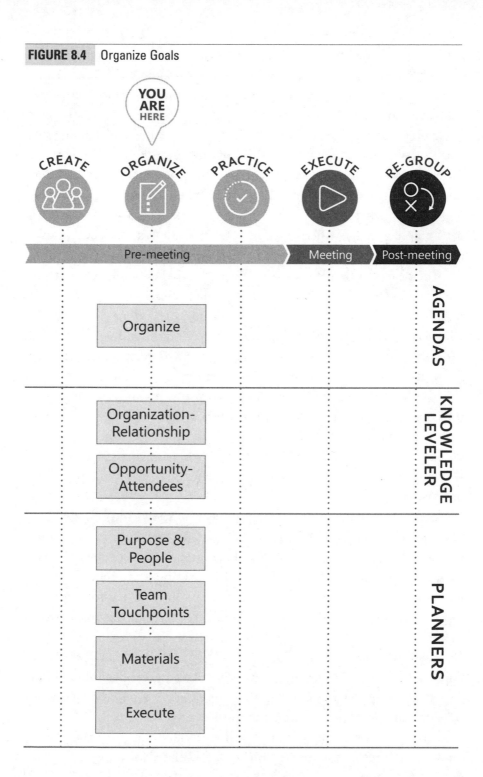

customer information as the group gets closer and closer to the pitch. On some teams, nearly all customer information resides with one person. There are many instances where this is not the case. Your organization's relationship with this customer may span across different parts of your organization and, within each, there are different leads and different client contacts. In this circumstance, knowledge leveling is done to accomplish the same goal, but the process is trickier and may involve both core and extended group members. There are commonly large gaps in what knowledge you have for the launch meeting weeks or days before go-time. These gaps help team members focus action over that time period to collectively fill those gaps.

The planning element acknowledges that there is a project management component to leading a selling squad effectively. Coordinating team touchpoints, materials, and other logistics, done well and in advance, avoid distracting eleventh-hour drama and embarrassing mistakes. Leveraging technology and extended team members can strengthen your team's ability to plan, monitor, and execute its activities.

The final element to cover during team touchpoints is practice, or rehearsing. The connection between practice and an excellent performance is clear to artists yet, in my experience, not as widely embraced among salespeople. In fact, I sat down with a few artists in my network to get a sense of just how much rehearsal occurs before a final performance.

Evan Weinstein is a television producer on shows like *The Amazing Race*, which has won 10 Emmy awards for Outstanding Reality–Competition program. On this show, there are no actors, but you can imagine the logistics that are involved in staging and taping multiple teams following different paths at different times to try to reach the same destination. For Weinstein's team, the process for testing key elements for one episode can begin 8 to 10 weeks prior to taping. (Dalis, Interview with Evan Weinstein, Aug. 7, 2015) While much of the show appears organic and improvised, there is in fact a great deal of planning and practice involved in creating that appearance. Similarly, a successful pitch should have that same natural, yet organized, feel.

Another artist I spoke with was Raymond Rodriguez, the associate artistic director for the Silicon Valley Ballet. Not only do each of the 32 dancers train and prepare individually, the full company of performers also meets for show-specific rehearsals. This process begins five weeks in advance of opening night and runs from 9:30 a.m. to 5:30 p.m. each weekday. That totals roughly 175 hours that Silicon Valley Ballet's artists spend together before a production. (Dalis, Interview with Raymond Rodriguez, Aug. 11, 2015)

A sales or customer meeting is not a performance per se, and does not require the intricate coordination that a TV or ballet production requires among production staff and performers. Several weeks or 175 hours of practice time is unrealistic and probably not even needed. However, there is a lot of room between 175 and 0 hours. How much practice time would your team need to deliver the sales pitch you need to win the business—more than 1, fewer than 10? How will you decide?

For an Organize meeting specifically, let's look at what bases should be covered on knowledge leveling, planning, and practice?

Knowledge Leveling

You've qualified and decided to pursue an opportunity that is going to require including others to win. If this is a strategic account, there may be a formal account team that includes representatives from across your organization's lines of businesses; and you may have an established account planning process. At the other extreme, there are times that prospects and opportunities appear quickly and you find yourself with very little information and no prior history with the customer. While your access to stakeholders in either case may be limited, the availability of information in the public domain is enormous thanks to the Internet. So, what information needs to be shared with your colleagues who join your selling team?

I find that what gets shared by leaders with their teams, in practice, runs a wide range from a few crumbs to the whole bakery. The common thread among most knowledge sharing is that it takes the form of an information dump rather than a thoughtful parsing of need-to-knows. Common mistakes include sending a link to the buyer's website or copying and pasting large sections from company materials. Leaving it to your colleagues to look it up themselves or sift through tons of text is not only inconsiderate; it's likely to result in team members reading little if anything in advance, and arriving at your very important meeting with insufficient knowledge about the client. Internal colleagues and external partners who agree to join your selling efforts have priorities and responsibilities that may not align with yours, so it is important to aim for efficiency and relevance to properly and efficiently prepare them for your high-stakes meeting.

There is no shortage of information that could be shared. In my experience, the Knowledge Leveler form in Figure 8.5 contains what should be shared so that your team can better understand how they fit into the client's buying or thinking process, and how their capability fits within your larger presentation.

KNOWLEDGE LEVELER: ORGANIZATION-RELATIONSHIP

- **Name and brief description:** What works is a few sentences that give your team members a flavor for the person or organization—their industry/sector and role within it.
- **Mission:** What is the client's aspirational mission? At times, these statements are check-the-box statements filled with corporate jargon. For some people, families, and organizations, they can be a rallying cry; knowing both the mission and language used can help your team members tie a capability to that mission.
- **Goals:** If you have learned of specific metrics, such as earnings-per-share growth (for a publicly traded company) or percentage reduction in disease cases (for a nonprofit), against which the client is measuring progress, these too can be helpful as your team thinks through how to position key messages in a way that will resonate with stakeholders.
- **Key lines of business:** It is not necessary to be exhaustive in listing every branch of the family or corporate tree, department, and trademark. Where does the organization or person generate most of its business? How does the customer organize itself? For example: "XYZ Healthcare has three main facilities and, within these, is known for five specialty areas (name them)."

FIGURE 8.5 Knowledge Leveler: Organization-Relationship

KNOWLEDGE LEVELER
ORGANIZATION-RELATIONSHIP

Client Name

Mission:

Goals:

DIVISIONS

BUSINESS WON

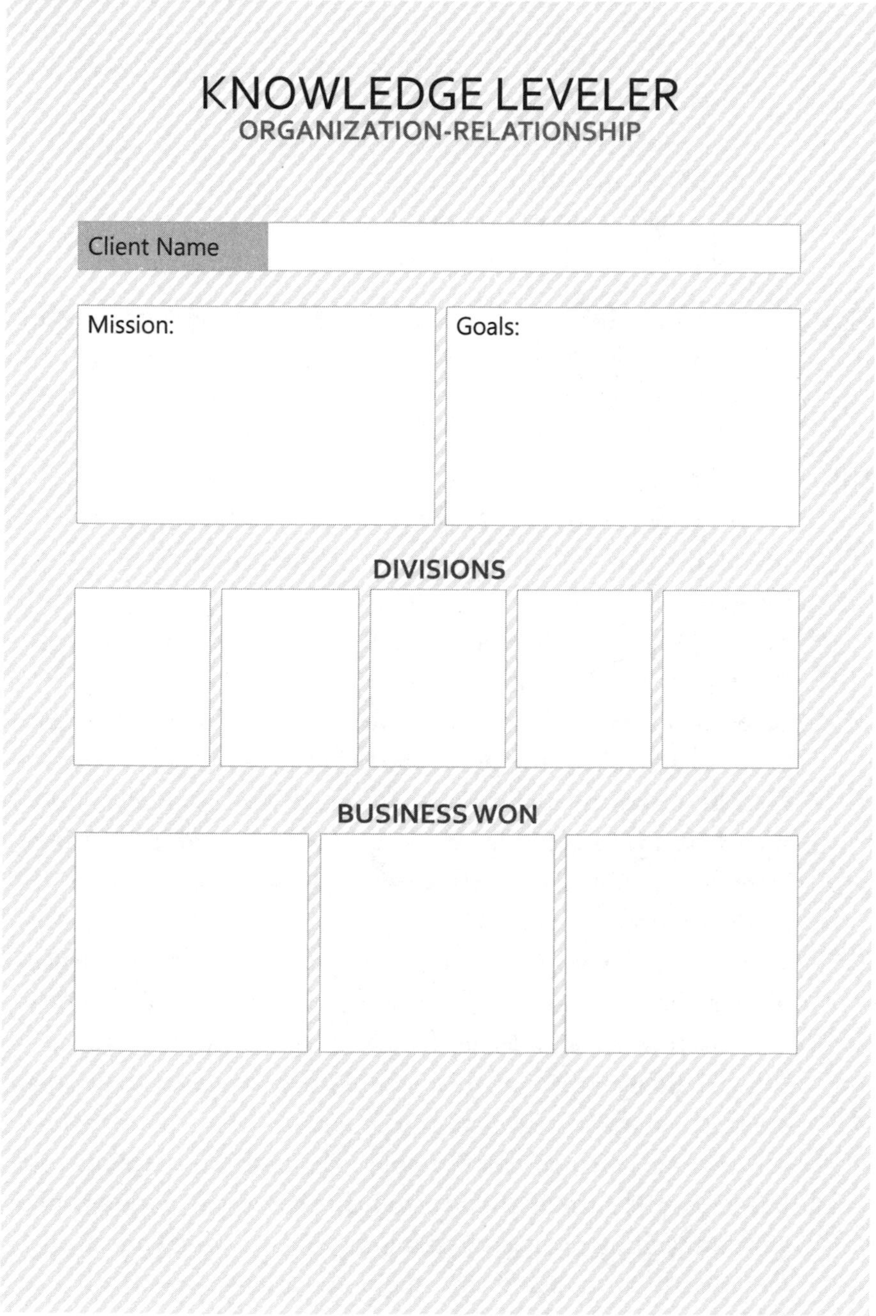

- **The relationship:** Provide brief snapshots of recent work that's been done by your company for this organization. For each, include:

  - Scope of the work
  - Size, in terms understood by your team
  - Status: completed or in-process
  - Outcomes: what was the result
  - Connection to client's key lines of business

Figure 8.6 shows the knowledge leveler for the opportunity and attendees.

THE OPPORTUNITY

- **Description:** Describe in a few sentences, using language your colleagues will understand, what opportunity is on the table.
- **Scope:** What are the parameters, elements, components of the deal?
- **Size:** Define size in a way that's meaningful to your team members, such as assets, revenue, volume, and so on.
- **Decision-making body:** Who will make the selection decision? It may be a group of individuals, a formal selection or steering committee, a board of directors or trustees, or a committee under a board.
- **Issues:** What have you learned from your contacts about what's driving them to consider the cost and risk of a change? I worry as a coach when team leaders respond to this question with "They're doing a search." As a team leader, you want to be able to understand and convey to your team why the customer is considering a change. For example, the committee has lost confidence in the current provider to help their organization comply with impending regulatory changes. This will help your team members to formulate their value propositions.
- **Connection to key lines of business:** Customer organizations can be large and complex. Helping your team locate where

FIGURE 8.6 Knowledge Leveler: Opportunity-Attendees

KNOWLEDGE LEVELER
OPPORTUNITY-ATTENDEES

Client Name

This opportunity:

Why qualified:

Why do this?
Why now?
Why with us?
Why with them?

DIVISIONS

Decision-making body:

ATTENDEES

among the key business lines this opportunity fits simplifies the picture for them. For example:

> Our flux capacitors will be used by Amalgamated Industries' Construction Division to reshape time and space, so that they can come in under budget and on time in 100 percent of their projects.

- **The reasons this opportunity is qualified:** Recalling the four Why's to qualify from Chapter 3, share the strength of your convictions behind:

  1. Why must the customer do this? Connect the opportunity to the organization's mission and goals, as stated on the "Organization-Relationship" page.
  2. Why must the customer do this now? Same consideration as above.
  3. Why they should do this with you?
  4. Why you want to do this with them?

- **Their attendees:** For each buyer stakeholder attending the meeting, convey to your selling team:

  - Connection to key lines of business: Include title, plus key line of business with which they are aligned. Point out if their role crosses lines of business, such as for senior management or procurement. This will help your team visualize their counterparts' roles in the client organization and how they connect to one another.
  - Connection to past work: In snapshots cited above, point out which ones they were involved with and in what role.
  - Role on decision-making body: What role do they play on this committee, board, or group? You may choose to keep this as simple as: leader, member, or advisor.
  - Support strength: How strong is this person's support for your organization relative to competing organizations—positive, neutral, negative, or unknown?
  - Decision drivers: Whatever you have been able to discover about each stakeholder's key drivers should be shared with

your team so they can emphasize these points, where appropriate, in their comments

- Personal interests: For each attendee, what have you learned through your research that would allow your teammates to forge personal connections at timely moments—before, during, and after the meeting? For example, a recent trip to New Zealand, board member for local children's hospital, or avid mountain biker.
- Participation: Will this person be at the meeting live, or virtually via audio or video link? Knowing this will allow your team to simulate this during your Practice session and to be well prepared for the actual meeting dynamics at go-time.

Your reaction after reviewing the Knowledge Leveler in Figures 8.5 and 8.6 may be something like, "How and when am I supposed to do be able to do all of that?!" Assuming you have qualified this opportunity, and carry that conviction in recruiting colleagues to the sales effort, your investment is already sizeable. Taking the time to level knowledge among selling squad members, in a format that will help them prepare and perform, may be the "lean at the tape" type of difference that will help you win a highly competitive sale.

You will find that using the Knowledge Leveler and other templates in this book will keep things simple and on point. Just as you would when communicating with a customer, breaking information down into pieces—or "chunks" as the behavioral psychologists call them—increase the likelihood that your team will read it, and your investment of time will pay off.

Planning

The project management component of selling squads is one that in my experience effective team leaders come to appreciate—not because they love it, but because early planning avoids last-minute distractions that take their team's focus away from where it needs to be to execute a successful sales meeting.

I have included planners to help you coordinate your team's work together during the Organize stage. Let's start with going deeper into Planner 1, which you started during the Create stage.

1. PLANNER 1—PURPOSE AND PEOPLE

- **Goals:** Objectives establish intent for a significant client touchpoint. (See Figure 8.7.) That old adage that applies here is, "If you don't know where you're going, any road will get you there." Both well-established and virtual teams make some common mistakes here, including:

  - No objective
  - An objective set only by the salesperson leading the effort
  - Team has competing objectives
  - A weak objective

  It is not tough to spot the team that has fallen into one of the traps above. In fact, it can show up in the opening moments of a meeting, as soon the handshakes are over.

  A strong objective focuses and aligns your selling squad. It has the same effect as a shopping list in a store: optimizing time and money, and putting you in the best position to accomplish what you came for. Solid objectives meet four criteria. They are:

  1. Detailed: What commitments or feedback are you seeking?
  2. Visible: What must the client(s) do or say to confirm the commitment or feedback you are seeking?
  3. Timing: Within what period are you seeking that commitment or feedback?
  4. Shared: The team is aligned on the above.

  Discussing objectives early in your preparation calls or meetings gives you an opportunity to resolve any differences that exist among teammates. If you don't budget time to hash this out in advance, this might just happen when the team goes live in front of the client. Clear and aligned objectives

FIGURE 8.7 Planner 1: Purpose & People

PLANNER 1
PURPOSE & PEOPLE

Our meeting objectives:

CORE TEAM MEMBERS

Role:

Role:

Role:

Role:

EXTENDED TEAM MEMBERS

Role:

Role:

Role:

also enable the team to arrive at an important meeting better prepared.

For example: Let's say that your team is preparing to meet with a prospective client for an early stage discussion. If your team's (weak) objective was to get another meeting with this client, you might close the meeting by asking for another appointment, with the likely next step that you will check calendars and reconnect. Inefficient.

Alternatively, imagine that for the same meeting your team's (better) objective is:

> To gain the prospect's commitment for a follow-up meeting over the next two weeks, to go deeper into the project's scope and specs, with the key stakeholders in the line of business, IT, and procurement.

What could your team now do in advance?

1. Check your calendars for mutual availability, and come to the meeting prepared with days and times that work for the team members needed for the follow-up meeting.
2. Work with client contacts in advance to understand who from their organization would be important contributors to a deeper conversation. This would allow the team to be specific in gaining commitment for meeting details.
3. Think through the outline of what an agenda might look like, and what value the client would gain from that next conversation.
4. Decide who will ask for the meeting, and how he or she will describe and ask for it.

- **Roles:** Who from the core group will be playing what role in the pitch—leader, subject matter expert, technical expert, senior, junior, and so on. You may recall that this was something you thought about when building your selling squad. It's important to put it to paper in the team's shared document as a reminder that, regardless of what roles and titles we have in the company, we may play a different role in the sales meeting. Also be sure to note who will be participating live and who will be connecting virtually and through what medium. Knowing this will allow you to prepare for it.

You should also highlight who from the extended team will be supporting the core team and in what capacity—i.e., materials, logistics, coach, faux client, and so on.

2. PLANNER 2—TEAM TOUCHPOINTS

Coordinating calendars for preparation among busy professionals can feel impossible at times. What helps is getting a jump start on this and involving team members. (See Figure 8.8.) This role can be a great one for a member of the extended group who is highly organized or someone who is being groomed as a future selling team leader. Increase your time efficiency by leveraging easy tools such as Microsoft's Outlook calendar to scope out in advance of the launch meeting the time blocks that seem to work for everyone. At the launch meeting, try to nail down possible dates and times for a minimum of four team touchpoints:

1. Additional Organize calls or meetings: A week or so before go-time, this touchpoint allows the team to do some knowledge leveling and to check in with one another on the state of their preparation before the in-person Practice meeting.
2. Practice meeting: This is a full-on, in-person practice (rehearsal) session. For teams that are geographically dispersed, this meeting can only feasibly happen the day prior to go-time. Teams that are geographically closer to one another or even in the same office are well served by scheduling more than one "Set" session and conducting these a few days prior to go-time; the extra breathing room allows for greater creativity and willingness to experiment with different sequencing, phrasing, and roles; and to address any open issues.
3. Execute meeting: This is your team's last-minute huddle and client meeting logistics.

FIGURE 8.8 Planner 2: Team Touchpoints

PLANNER 2
TEAM TOUCHPOINTS

	ORGANIZE	PRACTICE	EXECUTE	RE-GROUP
Date				
Time (start/stop)				
Location or Dial-in				
Scheduled				
Coach needed				
"Client" panel needed				

4. Re-group meeting: To debrief and plan, schedule this meeting for immediately or soon after the pitch. Advance planning ensures the full team will be available.

3. PLANNER 3—MATERIALS

As with scheduling meetings, collaborate early on a plan to develop, produce, and deliver materials to give your team the best chance of arriving at the meeting with the right materials and media, in good form. With customer knowledge now leveled, think through together what materials are relevant—presentation components, agenda, media (pitch books, projector, tablets), white papers, agreements, and so on—and plan accountabilities for each. (See Figure 8.9.)

A few words on the importance of a customer meeting agenda. (See Figure 8.10.) You will want to begin blocking out with your team the elements of the customer meeting, from opening to closing; and for each section, how much time should be budgeted and who on the team will take the lead.

There are two common mistakes that can happen at this point: (1) there is no agenda or (2) the team uses the pitch book's table of contents as the meeting agenda.

No agenda—written or verbal—suggests no preparation and no game plan, causing the client to become disengaged and to question the time committed to a meeting. This also gives the customer permission to create their own agenda, which might not work for you and your team.

A pitch book's table of contents tends to make for a poor meeting agenda, and here's why. The table covers the points in your presentation. Assuming these are all focused on you—your organization, your team, your capabilities—you can expect your team to do most of the talking and the client team to be largely disengaged.

Agendas that are in sync with buyer stakeholders are focused around their organization's priority goals, challenges, initiatives, and more. If your industry and organization will allow you to, it is best to align your materials with the client's goals. From my work with companies in the regulated financial services industry, I know that customizing

FIGURE 8.9 Planner 3: Materials

PLANNER 3
MATERIALS

Owner	
Due Date	

	DESIGN	PRODUCTION	DELIVERY	COMPLETE
Presentation				
Media				
Agenda				
Agreements				
Thought leadership				
Contact info				
Other				

FIGURE 8.10 Example of Client Meeting Agenda

Amalgamated Industries
MEETING AGENDA

Title	Orals Presentation
Location	Happy Valley, PA
Date	June 15, 20XX

START	END	TIME	ITEM	KEY PITCH PAGES	PRIMARY
1:00 PM	1:00 PM	0:05	Open		Bob Gage
1:05 PM	1:10 PM	0:05	Agenda Check		Bob Gage
1:10 PM	1:25 PM	0:15	Needs check		Bob Gage
1:25 PM	1:40 PM	0:15	Capabilities in area A	6, 11	Jane Tracker
1:40 PM	1:55 PM	0:15	Capabilities in area B	14	Vijay Ahmad
1:55 PM	2:10 PM	0:15	Capabilities in area C	17, 19, 20	Anita Xi
2:10 PM	2:25 PM	0:15	Q&A		Bob Gage
2:25 PM	2:30 PM	0:05	Close		Bob Gage
	TOTAL	**1:30**			

Amalgamated Industries
CONFIDENTIAL

presentation materials can be a nonstarter. Materials that are available to salespeople are the output of a review process that is designed to ensure regulatory compliance. If there is no flexibility in presentation materials, consider developing and bringing an agenda as a separate document. In less formal settings, sliding your agenda across the table over lunch won't do much to keep folks comfortable. At least, come prepared to articulate your proposed agenda verbally.

Breaking down your agenda into two components—topics and time—allows you to check in with client stakeholders on both in your opening. Winning teams discuss and debate the agenda in advance to make sure it reflects the knowledge gained up to that point in the team's client discussions. It also allows the team to assign ownership over who will review and check on the agenda and time, and how changes to these will be handled, in the meeting.

Make sure to budget time on your agenda for questions and answers and to close. The proper amount of time is driven by the total time allotted for the meeting. At a minimum, teams are well served by covering all other points 10 minutes prior to the stop time agreed to. This allows the team five minutes each to at least check for open questions and to close thoroughly.

4. PLANNER 4—EXECUTE

Planner 4 allows the team to begin sorting out, as early as the launch meeting, logistics and responsibilities for presentation or meeting day. (See Figure 8.11.)

AGENDA: ORGANIZE MEETING

As your selling squad's leader, you will likely be running the meetings or calls for each team touchpoint. So, it's worthwhile to plan those agendas in advance, starting with your Organize meeting or calls.

We discussed the importance of an Organize meeting. Depending on the significance of the pitch or meeting for which you're preparing, you might also wish to schedule one or more Organize calls. (See Figure 8.12.) This allows the team to benchmark the state of their

FIGURE 8.11 Planner 4: Execute

PLANNER 4
EXECUTE

TEAM MEET-UP

Date		Time Start	
Location		Time Stop	

RESPONSIBILITIES

Team members			
Transportation			
Client team focus			
Materials/media			
Technology			
Personal technology			

FIGURE 8.12 Agenda 1: Organize Meetings or Calls

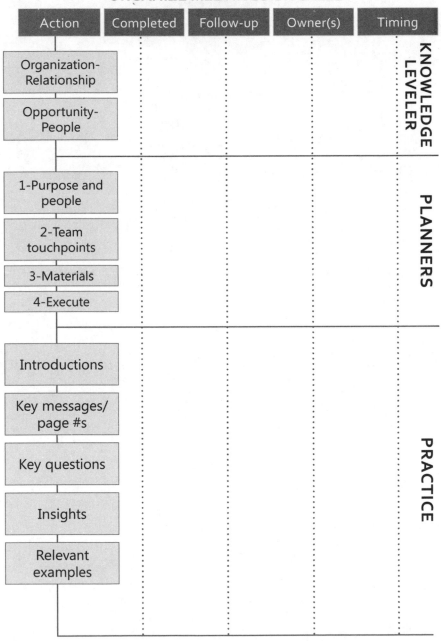

preparation. Allocate time to knowledge leveling, planning updates, and even practice. I like to include a discussion on meeting objectives as part of the planning process, to ensure that the customer meeting agenda reflects what both the client and your team want to accomplish. Meeting objectives should meet the SMART criteria: specific, measurable, action-oriented, realistic, and time-bound. By engaging your team in thinking through what they would like to close on, you will enable them to focus more on outcomes and less on what information they can push out during their section of the meeting. The practice component of your Organize meeting is not a full run-through. Quick round robins on how people will manage introductions and key parts of their value proposition allow the team to get aligned, share feedback, and sharpen rough edges.

Planning your selling squad's Organize, Practice, and Re-group touchpoints as much in advance as possible ensures the best attendance and avoids rebooking travel arrangements, which can be costly.

Pre-practice

Using the Organize meeting agenda, the knowledge leveler, and the planning tools will keep everyone grounded and on point. If you have time during your launch meeting, you might consider budgeting 10 minutes or so for a pre-practice session. It ensures readiness, and sends an important signal that while practicing in front of colleagues can feel awkward at first, it is essential to getting better and gaining a successful outcome.

So what could you possibly practice without presentation materials and having just shared what knowledge exists about this opportunity? Here are some areas you might consider test-driving while the team is together during an Organize meeting or call:

- **Introductions:** Avoid an early opportunity for fumbling and instead get ready to start the positive momentum early. If you like to introduce your teammates in a meeting, allow them to hear and react to how you plan to do that. If you prefer to have teammates introduce themselves, ask them how they might introduce their role in this meeting or engagement if your team is successfully awarded the business, and set a benchmark such as 30 seconds or less. You will recall that effective teams create feedback loops, and here is another one. As each member runs through his or her introduction, feedback should be given by the team. (Remember, think: balanced, specific, and honest in giving feedback. And seek to understand and not judge when you receive it.) The team shares feedback so the person can refine his or her comments and timing. Then sort through what sequence you will use, and run through it two or three times. This is a short and easy way to get on a path to building early momentum in the client meeting.

- **Key messages:** You've selected people to join you to contribute in certain ways. Given the territory they will need to cover in the actual meeting, it is helpful to begin road-testing some of those essential points and how they can be tied to the client's mission, goals, and obstacles. And this work has another benefit: it's an opportunity for collaboration, feedback, and support, so it builds teamwork.

- **Success stories:** Consider thinking through with core and extended team members what examples of similar work would resonate with the client. Discuss who should describe it, how, and at what point in the client meeting.

Also practice your team's feedback loop by creating an atmosphere where balanced, specific, and honest feedback can be given and received safely and effectively. You might also consider engaging your sales coach at your first Organize meeting. Richard Hackman, in *Leading Teams*, offers the following:

> A coaching intervention that helps a team have a good launch increases the chances that the track will be one that enhances members' commitment to the team and motivation for its work. (Hackman, 2002, p. 179)

Staging a well-coordinated Organize meeting allows you as a leader to gain focus and set a collaborative tone. In geometry, making a small shift in the angle at the source of a line makes a big difference on where the end point lands. Similarly, when you make small adjustments at the start of your time together, as in your Organize meeting, it can be a highly efficient way to put your group on a path to becoming a team that accomplishes an important objective.

CHAPTER 8

NOTES TO SELF

1. Key points to remember about the Organize stage of the selling squad Build Process:

   a. _____

   b. _____

   c. _____

2. Opportunity you are working today with a selling squad that is in the Create or Organize stage:

   _____

   What actions will you take, and by when, to complete:

   • Your knowledge levelers? _____

   • Your planners for:

      • Purpose and people _____

      • Team touchpoints _____

      • Materials _____

      • Execute _____

   • The agenda for your next Organize meeting or call?

   _____

3. To improve your long-term sales impact, you would like to:

   a. Stop: _____

   b. Start: _____

   c. Continue: _____

PRACTICE: FINDING YOUR FLOW

FIGURE 9.1 Practice Stage of a Selling Squad

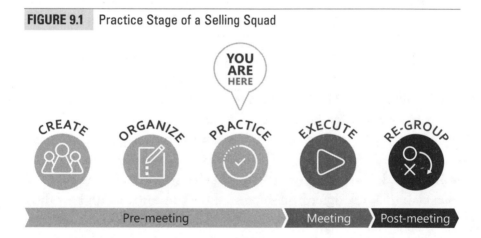

The Practice Session

Imagine this scenario . . .

The consulting firm's senior director was excited. In response to her firm's push for more business development activity, she had been doing more networking and as a result was referred an opportunity to do electronic discovery ("e-discovery") work with a large law firm in town. (This type of work involves searching electronically for case references rather than the old-school version of sending associates to the law library to pore through books.) Even better, the partner in charge of the vendor selection committee was a fellow alum and mentor from law school; and her firm was widely regarded as the No. 1 firm in e-discovery. *This is going to be fun,* she thought.

She reached out to her old law school friend and succeeded in getting an appointment to pitch their services. Her next call was to the head of the e-discovery practice in her firm, a really sharp technician with impressive academic and professional credentials, who agreed to join her on the sales call.

In the days that followed, the two consultants exchanged e-mails about the law firm and the opportunity, and agreed on what content should be included in their presentation book for the meeting. Two days before the meeting, they got together briefly to review the materials, agree on who would handle which section, and go over logistics for the meeting.

The meeting went on as planned and her old friend seemed impressed. The senior director looked forward to good news and what that would mean for her promotion prospects.

A few weeks later, her former classmate called with the disappointing report that the business had been awarded to a far smaller firm, one not listed among the industry leaders. She managed to keep her poise and ask about the rationale for the decision. The lawyer went on to explain that the other firm impressed the committee with how their solution and team would allow the firm to not only offload e-discovery; but also to weave together experts to support litigation teams, economists to assist their lawyers with assessing damages, and financial analysts who would place a value on the net impact to the firm. She regained her excitement and exclaimed, "Hey, we provide all those services too." "Well, maybe next time," he replied.

Where did she go wrong? According to Harvard professor and researcher on professional services firms Dr. Heidi Gardner, cross-discipline teams produce work that earns higher margins and greater client loyalty. (Gardner, *HBR*, 2015, p. 75) There is a big difference, however, between cross-selling and cross-discipline teams. Cross-selling, at the most basic level, involves introducing other lines of business to a customer. Cross-discipline solutions align with the customer's issue and span organization lines in their construction and implementation.

In this scenario, the smaller firm won the business by involving colleagues earlier and seeking access to stakeholders to understand the problem fully. They discovered that the law firm was having financial difficulties and was focusing its resources on winning two cases with large contingency fees. If successful, this would allow the firm to borrow more from its bank and avoid more severe options. After uncovering this information, the smaller firm was able to work together to create a holistic solution that was different from any it had provided in the past, and well beyond its e-discovery offering. The team got together two days prior to their meeting with the law firm and practiced. This enabled them to convey their solution in a way that appeared seamless to the client.

How many of the following traps do you recognize from your own work? How many of these did the senior director fall into, as her selling squad (of two) got ready for their final preparation before a pivotal meeting?

- **Not scheduling a practice session:** Given her relationships with the referral source and the committee head and her confidence in the firm's product offering, she assumed no practice was needed. The team missed an opportunity to collaborate not just in presenting facts about their firm and its e-discovery capabilities, but in understanding and developing a solution that lined up with the customer's challenges.
- **Having no game plan:** Cross-discipline solutions need to be presented in a way that is seamless to the client. Fitting together pieces that don't usually get assembled that way is tricky. For even more basic scenarios, going into an important customer discussion with no game plan ignores the complexity of selling with others.
- **Limiting preparation to talking things through:** This is the one I see most often in my coaching work. Practice is limited to talking through what presentation pages will be covered by

whom. The team does commit the time to get together, but only to discuss who will cover what pages. There is no practice and no feedback, so the team arrives at the meeting with no likelihood of being able to pull it off.

- **Absent team members:** Schedules and competing priorities make it tough to commit to practice time. Though this was not an issue for this senior director, in real life this can be especially true for those in demand, such as C-level executives, thought leaders, and rainmakers. As good as the missing person is in general, how that person will perform for this meeting and this team specifically is a huge unknown. We discussed this for the Organize meeting, and the same is true for a Practice session.
- **Scheduling an inadequate amount of time:** A brief preparation session leaves little room for the type of practice, feedback, and adjustments that result in excellence at go-time.
- **Not testing technology:** Technology such as PowerPoint, tablets, and audio- and videoconferencing can be great tools for elevating the impact of a presentation and allowing remote buyers and sellers to participate. Not practicing with them opens your team to embarrassment, distractions, loss of credibility, and wasted time during an important customer meeting or pitch.

Think about how small groups outside the selling world sync to perform. Brent Carter, lead singer for such bands as Tower of Power and Average White Band, talks about how the band may practice for a full day prior to going into the studio to record one three-minute track. Practice for a major tour begins a few weeks in advance, isolating and then bringing together the rhythm section, background singers, and, finally, the feature artist. (Dalis, Interview with Brent Carter, Aug. 6, 2015)

The day before opening night, the Silicon Valley Ballet stages a full-on dress rehearsal. This includes the full orchestra, makeup artists, costume designers, and the full cast of dancers. After the run-through, they break for lunch and then reconvene to share notes so they can make corrections before the audience arrives for opening night.

Think about any group performance—military, athletic, cultural, medicine—and you will recognize that teams practice together in a way that goes above and beyond the sort of role-specific preparation done by individual team members. Think of military maneuvers, team practice, dress rehearsals, run-throughs.

What a selling squad does is different from what a military unit, sports team, artist company, or surgical unit does. There is no face-off against an opponent, no paying audience to entertain, no patient to cure. Yet selling teams do face the same challenges in going from group to team. Without effective team preparation, they can only reasonably hope to be a group of experts. And how many times have you been part of a fantastic group of professionals with the best ideas . . . and still you lost?

So what does an effective Practice session look like for a selling squad?

Just as with your Organize meeting, you will leverage agendas, knowledge leveling, and planning during your team's Practice-stage touchpoint. (See Figure 9.2.) And there should be two parts to your team's practice, half-speed and full-speed; more on these in a moment.

Figure 9.3 shows an agenda for the half-speed portion, and Figure 9.4 shows the full-speed section of your Practice session.

Knowledge Leveling

As you did during your Organize meeting, provide time to allow team members to update one another about new developments, if any. Reflect on what you have learned since the team's launch meeting or call. What's changed about the client organization, opportunity, or attendees? What changes have there been to the selling squad? If nothing has changed, move on.

Planners

At this stage in the process, the date of your sales meeting is approaching and you have begun work on your planners. Here, your focus is

FIGURE 9.2   Practice Tools

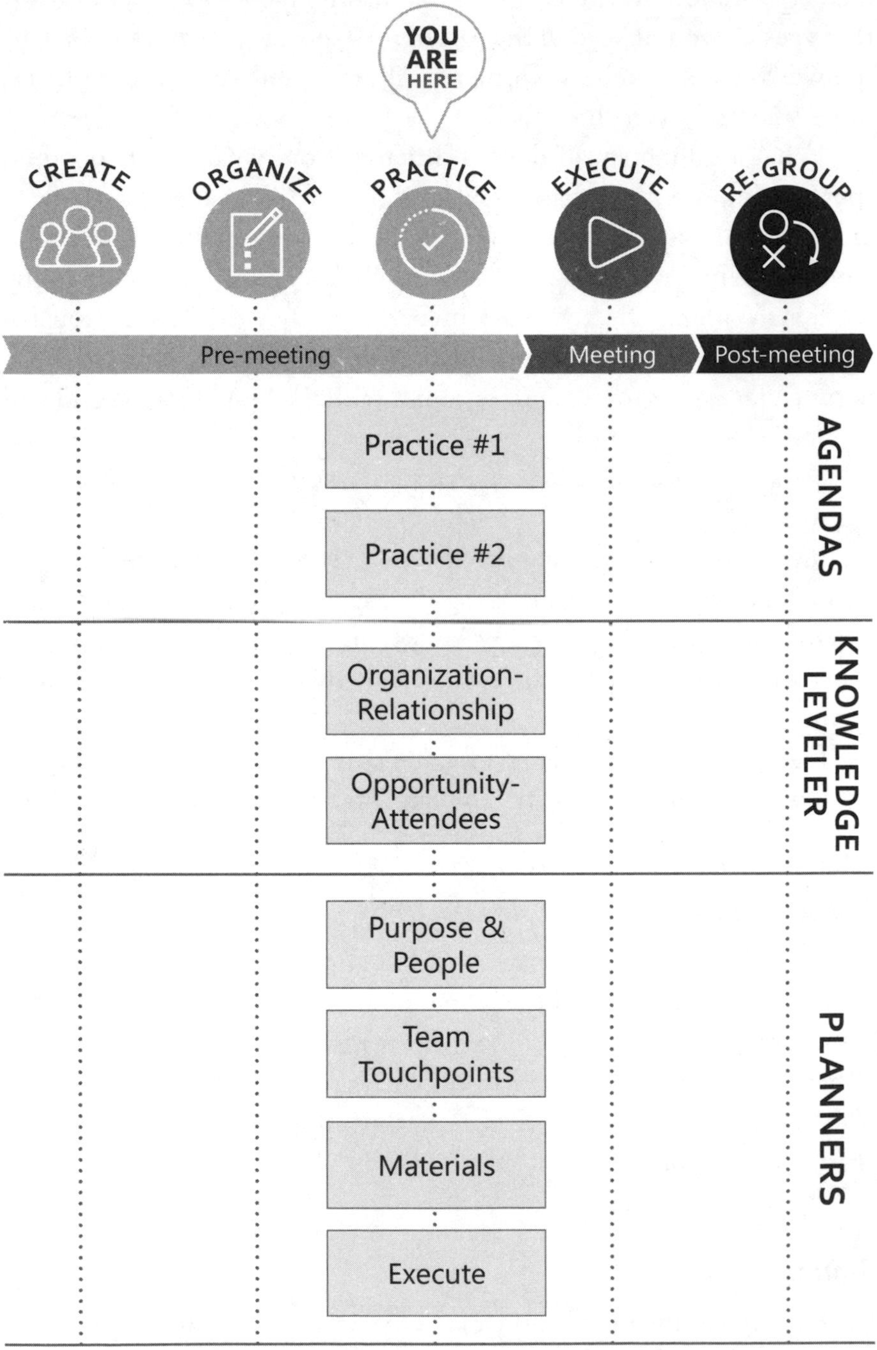

YOU
ARE
HERE

CREATE   ORGANIZE   PRACTICE   EXECUTE   RE-GROUP

Pre-meeting   Meeting   Post-meeting

| Practice #1 | AGENDAS |
| Practice #2 | |

| Organization-Relationship | KNOWLEDGE LEVELER |
| Opportunity-Attendees | |

Purpose & People	PLANNERS
Team Touchpoints	
Materials	
Execute	

FIGURE 9.3 Agenda 2: Practice #1 (Half-Speed)

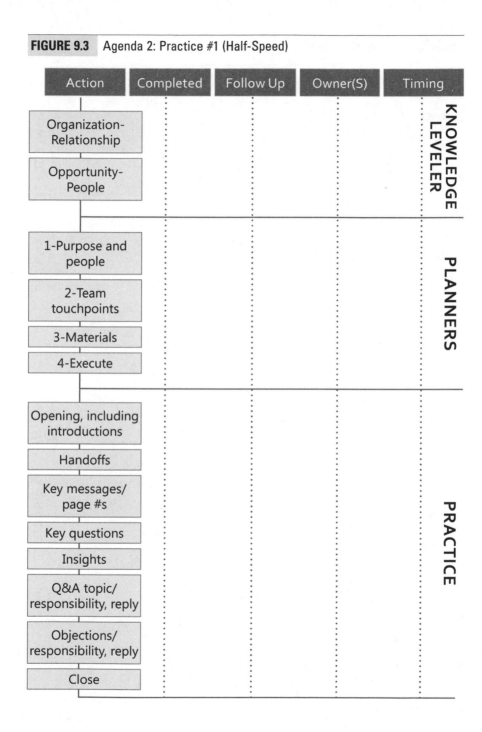

FIGURE 9.4   Agenda 3: Practice #2 (Full-Speed)

Action	Completed	Follow Up	Owner(S)	Timing	
Organization-Relationship					KNOWLEDGE LEVELER
Opportunity-People					KNOWLEDGE LEVELER
1-Purpose and people					PLANNERS
2-Team touchpoints					PLANNERS
3-Materials					PLANNERS
4-Execute					PLANNERS
Opening, including introductions					PRACTICE
Handoffs					PRACTICE
All sections					PRACTICE
Q&A topic/responsibility, reply					PRACTICE
Objections/responsibility, reply					PRACTICE
Close					PRACTICE
SOS signal					PRACTICE
Unexpected events					PRACTICE
Seating plan					PRACTICE
Dress code/formality					PRACTICE
Hygiene/selling energy					PRACTICE
Technology					PRACTICE

on updating your planners (and plan) so they're factoring in any new developments:

- **Planner 1—Purpose and people.** Take the opportunity to review your goals and team lineup, discussing adjustments as needed.
- **Planner 2—Team touchpoints.** What updates are there for subsequent team interactions, including your Re-group meeting?
- **Planner 3—Materials.** Review status updates on production, delivery, and ownership of materials—including the presentation, agreements. and collateral pieces and the status of technology such as tablets and audio or video links, if they are being used. You should also refine your agenda for the customer meeting, including a final review of agenda topics, timing, and coverage of key pages.
- **Planner 4—Execute.** A successful pitch or meeting begins in your planning. Because your Practice session is likely to be scheduled close to the date of your sales meeting, this is a good time for your selling squad to visualize what will happen on that day. That is not to say it should be scripted in minute detail and that there will be no surprises. In fact, if there is one certainty it is that your big meeting will be different from what you expect. Well-prepared teams are, in my experience, nimbler, more flexible, and more willing to go off-script than are teams who have rigidly prepared around a presentation document. So, review logistics and responsibilities for game day.

LOGISTICS

- **Team meet-up:** You should plan a team huddle before the meeting. Pick a time that's not too close to the beginning of the meeting and a location nearby the meeting site. Consider the wide range of travel mishaps—wrong address, flight delays, traffic, and so on. At a minimum, your meet-up gives the team a margin of error in collecting as a team, allows everyone to get introduced or reintroduced, and lets everyone walk into the client meeting feeling and looking like a real team. The simple act of driving together to the client meeting can help the team feel and look more unified, get in some final practice or coaching, or simply get more comfortable with one another as people, which will help with both this and future meetings you work together.

The team meet-up, at its best, also allows the team to do a high-speed talk-through of the presentation or meeting. You've see athletes before a big moment, sitting on the sidelines with their eyes closed, making partial gestures to mimic the moves they will make in full form and intensity when the gun goes off. From open to close, a quick talk-through allows the team to visualize their meeting plan, including handoffs and key points, moments prior to the real thing.

- **Client meeting logistics:** Make sure the team is crystal clear on the location of the actual meeting and the start/stop times. For those traveling separately, make sure you understand their travel plans and be prepared to provide directions or GPS coordinates. You should be prepared to print them out or provide links to them.

- **Dress code:** How do you want your team dressed? Coordinated outfits in your organization's logo colors would certainly draw attention. More importantly, how are the client's attendees likely to be dressed? Showing up to a young technology company in investment banker pinstripes and suspenders would be as poor a choice as assuming that a casual dress code for employees means your team should enter in jeans and Hawaiian shirts. Get client guidance on this. Also, broad definitions of business professional and business casual mean a range of things to organizations and people, including different members of your team. Be specific with your expectations about how dressed up or down they should be. And if you worry about one member of your team who enjoys making fashion statements—with expressive jewelry, socks, colors, cologne, and clothing—trust your instincts; be direct with the person prior to go-time and explain it in terms of what the client wants rather than as your opinion.

- **Hygiene:** Different cultures and people within those cultures have different norms for hygiene. Be sure to close any gaps between team member norms and the client's, prior to the meeting. Better to have an awkward conversation in advance than to distract a client stakeholder and risk losing the business.
- **Business cards:** Decide how contact information will be shared with the client in advance. Some organizations like to send a contact sheet with pictures and contact details in advance. Others include them with the presentation materials. Still others attach cards to a page in their pitch book.
- **Personal technology:** If you are a parent, what does it feel like when your children come to the table with their mobile device? It is surprising how many stories people share with me about colleagues who check their phones during sales meetings. They need to understand that it doesn't make them look important. They come across as arrogant and disinterested. Personal phones and tablets are to be turned off and tucked away during the meeting. Your team's focus if you are going to be successful needs to be where it belongs—not on other things people could be doing, but on this moment with this customer and with your teammates—from entering to exiting handshakes.

DIVIDE AND CONQUER

Work out Execute stage (meeting day) responsibilities among your team members. Who on the core or extended team will take the lead on:

a. **Arranging transportation:** This should be for all members who will be participating in the meeting.
b. **Setting up the room,** if needed
c. **Bringing materials:** This may need to be broken down further into items such as the agenda, the presentation books, thought leadership pieces, and agreements. If you're bringing tablets and/or hardcopy materials, like a pitchbook and agenda, someone should be tasked with distributing them to the client team.

d. **Connecting the technology:** The responsibility for hooking up a projector, a web connection, or audio/video link by default often goes to the team leader. The risk with that approach is that, when the team leader should be focused on getting the team ready to open, he or she is getting distracted, frustrated, and anxious. Other members of the team can easily play this role. Assigning this responsibility to someone other than the selling squad leader ensures that if glitches need to be sorted through, the rest of the team can begin their opening as planned and practiced.

e. **Bringing and troubleshooting the technology:** If you are using a laptop, a projector, or tablets for meeting attendees, who on your team will make sure they are in someone's bag and brought to the meeting? This is probably the biggest distractor on game day. Who on your team can be charged with lining up the IT contact at the client site, being a resource for client team folks who are struggling with their tablets, getting connected to the wireless, and getting your presentation materials cued up for whatever screen display, if any, is being used? This person should also road-test the technology in advance.

f. **Connecting with individual stakeholders on the client team:** This includes connecting with stakeholders, whether they are participating live or virtually, prior to or with their comments during the meeting. It is the responsibility of the individuals who comprise the selling squad to connect with the individuals who comprise the buying or client team. Consider how a basketball or football team assigns coverage for opposing players. To the extent you have been able to meet and learn about the stakeholders who will be present at the meeting, your team members should be tasked with connecting with specific people on the client team, armed with some facts that will make it easier for them to connect on site.

g. **Formulating a seating plan:** Given the venue, how will the team arrange itself so you can see both the client team and each other? Allow the economic buyer to sit first. Note where other key contacts sit relative to the economic buyer. Be willing to sit on different sides of a table and between client contacts if you're able to—without diving or using sharp elbows. This allows your selling squad to stay visually connected with one another. And be sure that each teammate is in direct line of sight to the stakeholders for whom they are accountable.

h. **Final comments to the team:** Whether these come from the team leader or a senior executive, sort out in advance who will be making the comments and what they will be. Encouraging and confidence-building statements around the theme of being excellent will enable the team to hit its highest potential in this high-pressure moment.

The responsibilities listed above can be assigned to individual team members, but some responsibilities are best shared by the team. Commonly these all fall to the salesperson, who can lose focus on the team's broader game plan and connecting with the client before an important sales meeting or pitch begins. Your selling squad should mutually commit to the following:

a. **Bringing their best energy:** Being focused and present on game day means bringing your selling energy. (This is covered in-depth in Chapter 17.)

b. **Understanding the degree of formality of the meeting:** Is this a formal pitch in a board room; an informal table discussion in the CEO's conference room; or an early stage meeting with several customer stakeholders? The level of formality can impact several choices, including core team members, agenda, dress, materials, technology, and seating arrangement.

c. **Understanding the degree of formality of the client team:** Based on your prior contact, is the culture an informal one where people are fun and laid back? Or is it more serious in both their dress and how they interact? The answer to these questions can affect how you and your selling squad decide to question, share ideas and recommendations, and interact with one another.

d. **Appreciating client sensitivities:** What terminology can you share with the team that resonates with the client? Likewise, what terms set them off? I recall participating in a pitch to

UPS early in my sales career. Our organization was a FedEx customer, so we automatically used that carrier to ship presentation and other materials. The senior salesperson on the account reminded people on the selling squad that any express packages were to be sent to the client via UPS. And any comments made during the meeting about delivery method of reporting should use the verb "UPS" versus "FedEx."

e. **Avoiding acronyms:** Another point to remind your selling squad about is to use words that are easily understood by client contacts. When I began working with one of the Big Four accounting and consulting firms as a sales coach, I was handed a glossary of terms so that I could understand their pattern of language. Acronyms make it easy for internal colleagues in a large, complex organization to understand one another. It is understandable how, with internal colleagues around one another on a selling squad, folks might forget that clients don't speak that language. Using industry and company jargon and acronyms are a quick way to create disengagement and get cut from a competitive bidding process.

f. **Preparing for unexpected events:** The one guarantee in a sales meeting is that the real event will be different from the one for which you and your selling squad prepared. So it's important to review curveballs you could see: abbreviated time, change in attendees, a client who seems disengaged, technology that doesn't work, and more. In addition, talk through how you might handle these as well as your approach for handling those not on your list.

Practice

Knowledge leveling and planning updates are important, but the focus of your Practice session should be, well, practice.

Consider dividing the time remaining for your Practice meeting into two parts: half-speed and full-speed practice. Half-speed practice is a walk-through of your presentation, and full-speed is a run-through. In all, a Practice session may encompass a full day. This can sound like an extraordinary investment. Keep in mind that for well-qualified and important opportunities, the goal is not to check the box. The goal is to accelerate the team's development through practice, in order to win. So, yes, it is a big investment.

HALF-SPEED PRACTICE

In theatrical productions, individual cast members spend weeks and more to memorize their lines and research their roles. At some point the cast is brought together for a read-through. The purpose is to give life to the ideas that seemed brilliant to each performer in their individual preparation as well as to, now, see how they sound and mesh together with those of the director and other players. Your selling squad's half-speed practice session is a walk-through of the content from start to finish, stopping along the way to share feedback and to make decisions that will strengthen the team's execution.

During your team's half-speed practice, walk through the closing summary, the asks, responses to possible resistance, and next steps. While nearly all selling teams give thought to how they will open, a much smaller number think through how they will close. Some reminders to sort out in your team's half-speed practice: Who will close? What commitments are being sought, and how will you ask for them in a way that leaves no doubt where you stand? What are the logical next steps, and who will chronicle them?

Your selling squad's half-speed practice is another chance to practice your team's feedback loop. We talked in Chapter 8 about how to give and accept balanced, specific, and honest feedback. Let's talk here about a process for managing multiperson, peer-to-peer feedback. As we will discuss in Chapter 11 during your selling squad's Re-group meeting, exchanging feedback is best done one-on-one and in a private setting so selling partners feel safe. Not managed, a group feedback session can feel like a pile-on. So use these guidelines to manage feedback during both your half-speed practice run:

- Stop for feedback after each section of the meeting or presentation—for example, after the opening, after each presenter, after question and answer, and after the close.

- Ask the partner(s) who played the primary roles during that section to assess themselves first. Guide them by using the same mantra of balanced, specific, and honest.
- Ask observers—core and extended team alike—to choose one priority strength and one priority area for improvement. If the customer meeting is the following day, coach people to go big on the positives and extremely light on the coaching point. There will probably be insufficient time to make major changes, but most people should be able to receive a minor coaching point, such as:

> You should consider pausing after the point you made about the charitable remainder trust structure. This is a complicated subject and one that can be a game-changer for this family given their philanthropic plans.

- Be consistent, so that the process and time used with each team member seems fair and equal.

FULL-SPEED PRACTICE

After lunch, conduct a full run-through of the meeting from open to close, including handling tough questions. No stops and no feedback until the end. Feedback rules remain the same. The team's dress rehearsal goes straight through from open to close.

In your full-speed session, practice bringing together the meeting in real time with no stops, and incorporating feedback from your half-speed session. Pay attention to some of the traps you worked on earlier. For example, ensure you've got five minutes or more at the meeting's end to properly close things up. Determine who is going to ask for the commitment, and how. Run through, as you did with insights, how your selling squad partners will overcome their instincts and allow the silence needed. Practice how you will leave that meeting clear on the action plan and which team members will take the lead in making sure the team's follow-up plan is aligned with that of the client stakeholders.

This is also the time for faux clients, pulled from the ranks of your extended team or colleagues outside the team (more on this in a moment), to take their seats or dial into an audio or video line, and get into character. Your coach, teammates, and "clients" should be capturing balanced, specific, and honest feedback throughout. Plenty of time should be budgeted following completion of the run-through to allow a robust sharing of feedback. The full-speed practice session ends with a review of action items each core member is committing to. If you brought a junior team member, whose abilities you feel confident in, this may be a great chance for that person to get some experience running through an initial pass at what he or she captured from the faux clients during the full-speed practice. You and the team can fill in any gaps, and check in with the "client" for completeness on not just the actions and accountabilities, but timing. Remember to convey enthusiasm and confidence in what is agreed to.

PRACTICE COMPONENTS

The purpose of both your team's half-speed and full-speed practices is to isolate and sharpen key parts of the sales meeting. These include:

- **Opening:** Run through how introductions will be handled individually and as a team. Repeating the introductions flow until the team finds its groove is a good use of practice time because it prepares your team to start off strongly during the actual meeting. This adds to the team's confidence and the momentum at the time members need it most.
- **Handoffs:** Beyond introductions, you will want to practice handoffs between members—i.e., subject and speaker transitions—as you go through the half-speed session. To use a basketball analogy, every pass is an opportunity to lose possession of the ball. Handoffs to and from colleagues who are participating virtually can be even trickier. So, work through and ideally practice when they will happen, from whom to whom, and how. These can be great opportunities for the salesperson to play a role between the open and close, or for your specialists to demonstrate teamwork.

- **SOS signal:** Teams that sell together regularly develop a rhythm and intuitive signals or looks that keep them on track and aligned. Given the realities of today's selling environment, most selling squads don't have the time to develop these organically. So how do groups that come together infrequently, or only for one important client or prospect meeting, explicitly develop a signal that is implicit for intact teams? If everyone is participating virtually, using a chat box can be an effective way for selling partners to signal to one another. Avoid allowing these sidebar chats to become your primary focus and to be directed at an unintended person. For in-person meetings, when I ask teams how they will signal to one another that someone is going off-track, the most common refrain is they will give that person a swift kick under the table. Not likely, so let's be sure to work out something realistic that (1) is visible to, and can be used, by everyone and (2) is subtle enough that it won't shake a teammate or distract a client.

  This reminds me of a time that I, always the coach, was preparing with my wife for our first meeting with our daughter's boyfriend over dinner. When nervous, my wife, Sandy, tends to ramble. So we discussed the idea of an SOS signal in the car to avoid this, and all I could come up with was the word *bluebird*. So as we got to a point in the dinner conversation where Sandy was rambling, I turned to her and whispered, "Bluebird." We both blurted out laughing and were forced to reveal to our daughter and her boyfriend our pathetic SOS signal. *Bluebird* was visible, yes. Subtle? Not so much.

- **Key messages:** Each member will go through his or her key messages, including how they will reference any visuals. Again, this is key—this is not a talk-through, such as "I'll talk about how we. . . ." The team and the coach need to hear how each message will actually be communicated. The amount of time budgeted will drive the extent to which the coach and team can share feedback and allow that member a chance for a redo before moving on. Without key messages prepared and practiced, you risk missing the mark and running out the clock.

Coach team members—and this includes senior executives, specialists, and technicians—on key themes needed from them. These can be communicated in your Organize meetings or calls, so they can begin developing their comments. Have each team member practice delivering his or her portion of the presentation, or key messages in the meeting, in a way that (1) is linked to the client's objectives and (2) meets the overall meeting's time blocking. One other best practice: to establish your experts' credibility, they should practice beginning their section, taking one minute or less adding color on their experience, credentials, and/or approach.

■ **Insights:** Some have suggested that clients and prospects value a "challenger" personality. Delivering an insight can create new streams of conversation with customers, challenging their thinking on an issue and even their perception of your organization's capabilities. For example:

> According to your company's most recent annual report, Amalgamated's Construction Division has lost market share over the last three years due to high costs and slow project performance. This has hurt revenue and has created a need to turn the tide. According to research done by Dr. Emmett Brown, flux capacitors allow companies to shift the time-space continuum resulting in an 82 percent reduction in costs and a 310 percent increase in time within which a project can be completed.

Challenging a person's or group's thinking is a high-risk move, with potentially a big payoff. Your teammates must be aware of and realize the importance of the game plan. Many people, especially those who are not regulars at the selling table, are unaccustomed to and feel uncomfortable with silence. Their tendency will be to fill the void and, in the process, may destroy the opportunity for which you prepared. Effective teams are clued in and aligned, practice delivering the insight, and let the moment play out as planned—even if your only role is to be silent for a few seconds while one of the client contacts struggles with his or her response. If this is an essential moment in your sales meeting, it is worth practicing.

Delivered poorly during a client meeting, challenging a customer's thinking with an insight can mark a quick end to your opportunity. Here are some best practices on how to prepare and deliver an insight with resonance:

a. Insights are best received when trust and credibility has been established. In other words, they are highest when you have a solid track record of delivering on expectations. They are tenuous if this is your first meeting.

b. The insight must be based on research or experience that is current and credible.

c. The relevance to this client or prospect of the research or experience must be linked.

d. With the context set, this is a moment for a thought-provoking statement followed by a question for reaction.

e. Prepare for how you will react when the insight is either validated or invalidated by the prospect or client.

f. Sort out who on your team will deliver what insight and when. Then practice and decide what roles each team member will play—including silent ones —during these critical moments.

- **Silence:** How and why should you and your team practice silence? These can represent pivotal moments in a sales meeting. Imagine those times, as above, when you are leveraging an insight to change perceptions or thinking, asking a thought-provoking question, or negotiating fees. Silence conveys presence. The purpose of pauses is to shift the next move to the client's side of the table. Even those with many years of experience in sales meetings can feel awkward at those moments. Imagine how subject matter experts, technicians, juniors, and less experienced salespeople are likely to feel.

  In some of the most dramatic musical pieces, there are pauses that create anticipation as the audience holds its collective breath to see what will happen next. What would happen if the cowbell player couldn't stand it another second and began clanging before the rest of the band was cued to begin? Moment ruined, band out of sync.

In a sales pitch or meeting, it's ironic that most memorable moments can be the ones without words. We will discuss negotiating later on. What's important to note here is that silence must be practiced until the point that it can be reliably coordinated—from the moment of delivery to the moment it's designed to be broken. And you might want to remind people that holding their breath and biting their tongue can cause serious injury. Just breathe.

- **Question and answer (Q&A):** Many salespeople are comfortable asking checking questions toward the top of a meeting to assure the team's got it right. Once that is completed, many teams go into autopilot moving through each section as a generic capability dump—zero relevance, and with little engagement. One way to change this dynamic is to brainstorm thought-provoking questions with which experts can begin their section. Asked well, these questions will improve dialogue and engagement and allow the executive, specialist, or technician to increase the relevance of their comments even beyond what was practiced. This is an opportunity for the team to field and address both anticipated questions and curveballs.

In managing the Q&A section of a formal presentation, it's important to budget adequate time and play a zone defense— carving out likely topics and assigning them to team members. In reality as in a game, balls (or in this case, questions) can land between the zones. How will the team handle them? This is a great role for you as your team's leader. Field and clarify the question with the client first. This ensures the team answers the right question, and gives the team time to think through a response. Before passing the ball to one of your partners, make eye contact with her, seek positive affirmation, and then use her name before passing the ball. This ensures she will be ready to catch the pass. As part of your preparation, anticipate what questions or resistance you might encounter. Sort out who will handle what and how. For example, if your client's CFO or procurement officer makes a comment on how your fees compare to others under consideration, will you handle this? Will your team's senior leader? It is easy to see how with some preparation and practice this pass can be handled with confidence and skill.

- **Close:** Many salespeople struggle with how to close a meeting properly. Where some are overly aggressive, others are too passive. These tendencies get magnified in team-based sales meetings. The challenges in closing any sales meeting well include running out of time, failing to gain commitments, and leaving loose ends.

Now that you know the bases that need to be touched and how to conduct the practice in half- or full-speed mode, let's end with logistics for an effective Practice session.

WHO SHOULD BE THERE?

- **Core team:** Make attendance mandatory for members of the selling squad, or core team. The weight of this ask varies by individual on your team. For pivotal meetings with well-qualified opportunities, the difference between a win and a loss can be marginal. In some industries, such as wealth management for ultra-high net worth ($50 million+) families, this opportunity may be your only shot for several years.
- **Extended team:** Think through what contributing, or extended team, members can contribute to or gain from your Practice session. Junior members learn from watching more experienced people deliver both the flawless and the flubs. They are also capable of capturing feedback that others may miss.
- **Faux clients:** If the meeting is important enough, simulating client stakeholders adds a layer of reality to your team's preparation. Asking extended group members is the most convenient. The downside is that they may not have enough objectivity or seniority to challenge the selling squad. People outside the pitch team, including sales managers or other salespeople, may play the roles more realistically assuming they come to the

Practice session prepared. Some consulting firms maintain a list of retired partners who are willing and, by virtue of their experience, quite qualified to play this role. You may be familiar with the concept of a mock trial for lawyers. You're aiming to simulate real life. Whomever you choose to play the client stakeholders, be sure to provide to them in advance your knowledge leveler to enable them to understand the opportunity and people involved. They should sort out who will play the roles that will be represented in the real meeting. This preparation will allow them to be prepared to ask tough questions and call out missteps if they happen.

■ **Coach:** You may recall that your selling squad's coach may be internal such as a sales manager, or external such as a private sales coach on retainer. Who will be your selling squad's coach? You will remember that your coach should not only be available at moments as important as your team's Practice session, but should be skilled at capturing and delivering effective feedback. Because the coach will be providing this feedback in the moments prior to a pivotal client moment, with little time for adjustments, the feedback must be highly focused on what team members and the collective can reasonably change in the coming hours or days that will affect a win, instead of on general developmental issues, such as asking more open-ended questions or eliminating filler words such as "um." The purpose is to allow the selling squad to make simple final adjustments, especially ones that may prove to be the deciding factor in a tightly contested pursuit. Show me a team that doesn't want feedback, and I will show you a team that is operating with an objective other than to win.

Susan Wheelan, in *Creating Effective Teams*, referenced a study of 330 coaching intervention studies that found that feedback produced the biggest lift to group productivity. (Wheelan, 2010, p. 16) So who should you choose as your squad's coach? Core and extended group members have an important role to play in sharing feedback among themselves. They do not, however, serve well as coaches since they lack independence and may lack coaching skills. Some organizations have internal sales coaches. These professionals may come from sales or sales effectiveness backgrounds and, being independent from the pitch team, can be a strong option for effective coaching. Other organizations engage external coaches for just such events. Whether you choose an internal or external coach, make sure that person has the sort of experience on which to base his or her feedback so it is geared to helping you win.

Where Should Practice Sessions Be Conducted?

I find that selling squads typically want to meet in a conference room in their organization's local office. This is a logical move since it is free and available and may be familiar to some, if not all, of the team.

If that is the one and only option, work with it. If you have flexibility, read on.

Remember when you took your SAT for college? For most, those hours of preparation were logged in the safety and intimacy of your room or work area. And given the importance, you may have enlisted the support of a grown-up to quiet your siblings and pets. On exam day, however, you were confronted by a large, unfamiliar room with many strangers making all sorts of noise that you were unable to control.

The same is true for athletes at home and away games. In summer camp, I remember leading my basketball team as its point guard through our set plays during practice in our gym. We had a good team, and we knew our plays and our gym. For our first away game, we played a neighboring camp. Leaving the bus and entering their gym, we found unfamiliar sights, sounds, and smells. Very few familiar faces, the gym looked bigger and the baskets looked higher. And of course there was the crowd . . . as rousing in their boos against us as they were in their cheers for their team. None of our plays seemed to work that night and we were beaten badly.

According to Hendrie Weisinger and J. P. Pawliw-Fry in *Performing Under Pressure*, moments perceived as high pressure cause teams to perform far below their best as limited processing capacity in the brain is devoted to taking in and processing new information—such as the exam hall or the other camp's gym—rather than focusing on and performing tasks at or close to the team's ability level. (Weisinger & Pawliw-Fry, 2015, pp. 62–65)

For selling squads preparing for a pivotal meeting, it's fine to use a familiar place for your walk-through. To make the run-through as impactful as possible, try to simulate the conditions for the live meeting. This can include finding space in an unfamiliar part of your local office. Hotels can also be a good source of space. The point is that if the real meeting will take place in an unfamiliar space, your practice should take place in a similar and unfamiliar space. For instance, imagine how much more comfortable team members will feel on game day in the client's board room if they practiced in an unfamiliar conference room that is different from the one in which their weekly meetings are held.

Video-recording and playback is an incredibly powerful training tool for general presentation skills. In the lead-up to an important customer meeting, it can force presenters to get beyond their self-consciousness in the real meeting. In my experience, however, it can also jack up the team's nerves beyond an already elevated state. This effect is most acute with colleagues who are infrequently part of sales pitches but are set to play a key role in your meeting. Examples include senior executives, subject matter experts, and technical specialists. Playing with video, even on something as seemingly harmless as a mobile phone, risks hurting rather than helping individual and team confidence.

Engaging faux clients, as just outlined, is in my view a better way to simulate any self-consciousness people are feeling when they first present. Going through the team's full-speed practice session accomplishes the same purpose of enabling people to look outward rather than inward.

The feedback should be handled as it was with the half-speed run, with one exception. It should be conducted after the close is completed.

In summary, there is much to accomplish in your team's Practice session—knowledge leveling, planning updates, and, most of all, half- and full-speed practice sessions. This is a significant commitment of time and energy, especially given your team members' other responsibilities. You've worked hard to qualify this opportunity and build your team. A well-run Practice session gets your team aligned as a unit and prepared to execute at or close to the best of its abilities at go-time.

CHAPTER 9

NOTES TO SELF

1. Key points to remember about the Practice stage of the selling squad Build Process:

    a. _____

    b. _____

    c. _____

2. What actions will you take, and by when, to plan an effective Practice (half-speed and full-speed) session, to:

    - Update your knowledge levelers? _____

    - Update your planners for:

        - Purpose and people _____

        - Team touchpoints _____

        - Materials _____

        - Execute _____

    - Develop the agenda for your Practice session? _____

    - Manage logistics, including meeting space, food, technology links, materials, etc.? _____

    - Engage a sales coach? _____

    - Include faux clients? _____

3. To improve your long-term sales impact, you would like to:

    a. Stop: _____

    b. Start: _____

    c. Continue: _____

CHAPTER 10

EXECUTE: CARPE DIEM

FIGURE 10.1 Execute Stage of a Selling Squad

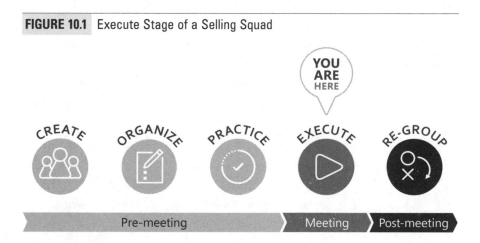

Picture this scenario . . .

A selling squad, comprised of four colleagues, arrived from four different locations for an important customer meeting, where they planned to challenge a stakeholder's thinking on a pending project. In the process, they hoped to get an opportunity to expand this customer's view of their firm's capabilities and to find work outside the one division that had used them in the past.

All four members had put in the time to prepare for this meeting and felt good about their chances. The meeting was set to begin at 2 p.m. and, as the time got closer, the three members who had arrived were getting increasingly anxious about the one who hadn't. It turned out that Bob, a key subject matter expert, had entered the right street address but the wrong town in his GPS app and was now racing to arrive on time.

They decided to begin shortly after 2 p.m., without Bob. The customer was understanding and welcomed them. After some small talk, there was a pause as the teammates smiled and looked at each other. At first nobody talked, then they all talked at once. After some nervous laughter, the account executive began the opening comments he had planned.

Bob eventually joined the meeting and did a capable job describing how his area had worked on similar projects in the past. The customer was engaged and asked many questions, and the team was able to describe their experience and ideas.

At 3 p.m., the ending time that was discussed, the customer stakeholder smiled and thanked the team. When the account executive tried to discuss next steps, the customer stood up and apologized; he needed to take a call. He promised to follow up with them soon. The meeting was over.

The Execute part of team selling can cause team member emotions to run the gamut, from exhilarated to debilitated, and everything else in between. And as you now are more aware of, the complexity factor goes way up with a team, because you are not only dealing with your emotions but also those of your colleagues.

Common Traps

Here are some common mistakes I have seen teams make during the Execute stage, including some of the missteps that even well-prepared teammates, like those above, make routinely:

- **Arriving late:** This offers no opportunity for your team huddle, and to get focused and unified.
- **Arriving from different locations:** It can be amusing for clients to watch team members that have not met before introduce

themselves to one another. Sometimes these introductions take place in the parking lot outside the client's conference room; occasionally they happen at the start of the meeting. Consider what this says to a customer, prospect, or partner about their importance and your organization.

- **Technical malfunctions:** These can include trouble projecting a PowerPoint deck, inability to find a Wi-Fi connection for an online demo, a poor audio or video link for virtual participants, and presentation materials that have been improperly loaded on tablets. Each of these can represent an exciting moment for the IT people in the room to go into trouble-shooting mode. However, they also take precious time away from the kind of dialogue that wins deals.

- **Missing materials:** Given the variety, numbers, and formats of materials you plan to bring, consider how easy it is to forget stuff back at the office.

- **Misunderstandings:** Without proper planning, there can be confusion about who was bringing what (and whom), meeting time, meeting location, and appropriate dress code.

- **Energy level:** Your crew may be tired from a long night of client work, preparation, or partying; sluggish from a poor night's sleep in an unfamiliar hotel room; or jacked up on coffee or XL-sized Monster or Red Bull extra boost energy drink. Or maybe they're suffering from a lunch of suspect sushi.

- **Pep talk:** Comments from a selling squad leader or a senior manager from your organization in the moments before you go live are important. The intent may be to be inspirational, but avoid adding pressure. Using phrases like "do or die" or "must win" could push someone on your team from nervous into frozen solid.

- **Business card poker:** While it is a nice gesture to have each team member personally hand cards to everyone around a board table, this can create a cluster and burn time in those key moments when the team should be getting settled, focused, and under way.

- **Mobile device use:** When not speaking, it is tempting for team members to sneak a glance at their mobile devices. Or forget to turn off the sound on that ring tone with snappy show tunes.
- **Not having or not using the game plan:** This includes some combination of overreliance on presentation materials, poor time management, sticking rigidly to an agenda at the expense of client engagement, and no closing.

How many of the above mistakes are familiar from prior sales pitches?

Now, think about the most effective team meetings you have participated in. What was happening? Each member of the team seemed dialed in—to each other and to the client stakeholders. There was a sense of creative tension, not overly relaxed and casual, not tight—because the moment mattered to them; they were each leaning in.

Brent Carter, lead singer for the Average White Band, describes how he knows when the band is in sync: "We're looking at each other, we're laughing and having fun, most important is that we're listening to what the other people are doing. That's when it comes alive." (Dalis, Interview with Brent Carter, Aug. 6, 2015) Think about your last selling team pitch. How closely were the members of the team listening to one another?

Another great example of effective teamwork can be found in ESPN's short film "E:60, Silent Night Lights," which documents the incredible story of an unusual high school football team. (ESPN, 2015) The California School for the Deaf, in Fremont, has a total of 450 students and runs from grades K to 12. The coaching staff and team are all deaf. Their 2014 game schedule included 10 games, all but 2 of which were played against hearing teams. How did they do? In their first five games, they beat their opponents by a cumulative score of 227-0. One of the players explained: "Deaf people have a heightened sense of sight; we see things that a lot of people can't. We sign fast. We communicate fast."

It's interesting that a team of scrappy high school boys, many of whom were born without a sense that most of us take for granted, are able to be so in sync with one another. That's what Execute is all about.

The Reasons Behind the Traps

What are some of the reasons that teams perform ineffectively in high-stakes meetings?

- **Pressure:** We covered this topic in Chapter 4. Hendrie Weisinger and J. P. Pawliw-Fry describe it as follows:

  > In most high-pressure situations, your life is not literally on the line, except for those who operate in high-risk environments—NAVY Seals, police officers, mountain climbers, air traffic controllers, emergency room medical staff. But on a primal level, the feelings and thoughts of pressure are similar: if you don't perform, you or others could be negatively affected, and you will be held back, you will not succeed. (Weisinger & Pawliw-Fry, 2015, p. 39)

  That do-or-die mentality may grip one or more members of your team.
- **Preparation:** By now you have come to appreciate how much preparation can be done for a high-stakes moment with a client, prospect, or partner. What would it look like in an extreme situation where, say, a selling squad arrives at a sales meeting with zero preparation time together? You have also hopefully come to see how team preparation, done well, will help each team member feel more comfortable and ready during Execute and, as a result, allow the team to perform at or close to its best.

Managing the Execute Stage

So what does an effective Execute agenda look like? You will find that your Execute planner serves well in this regard. (See Figure 10.2.)

- **"Execute" meet-up:** The complete selling squad meets at a point close to the actual client meeting location. Ideally this occurs two hours before the meeting's start time. This allows plenty of

FIGURE 10.2 Planner 4: Execute

PLANNER 4
EXECUTE

TEAM MEET-UP

Date		Time Start	
Location		Time Stop	

RESPONSIBILITIES

Team members			
Transportation			
Client team focus			
Materials/media			
Technology			
Personal technology			

time for late arrivals, getting reconnected as a team, and traveling the remaining distance to the meeting location. This is also an opportunity for any last-minute knowledge leveling, including checking your e-mail and news feed for any new intelligence gained. It is also a time for the team to do a rapid talk-through of the meeting flow, from start to finish, so that everyone is aligned in visualizing the game plan. And, who knows, maybe there's also a chance to fix a tie, wipe a crumb, or get rid of a stream of paper on someone's shoe.

■ **Execution:** Now it's time to execute on all that great work you and your selling squad did during Practice. Some quick reminders:

    a. Opening: To help your team start on the right foot and build momentum in the first moments of an important meeting:

        i. Make eye contact with one another to cue that you're ready to begin.

        ii. Take a nice healthy breath so that the first words the client hears come out smooth, resonant, and confident.

        iii. Run your introductions sequence just as you practiced.

    b. Handoffs: To ensure solid passes to one another and to demonstrate cohesive teamwork, combine eye contact and names before each handoff.

    c. "SOS" signals: To support one another:

        i. Use the signal (pen, glasses, the word *bluebird*) agreed to during your Practice session.

        ii. If that doesn't work, jump in at a pause, smile, use your colleague's name, and redirect with a question that will allow your partner to gracefully wrap up a point and pass the ball back to the client or to you.

    d. Flow: Once the agenda and time are clear and aligned with the client's interests during the Open, effective teams show purpose in covering and moving among the relevant topics in the time allotted. That means holding each other accountable to sticking to time frames, even if there are facts left unsaid.

e. Flexibility: To stay focused, recall:

   i. Almost 100 percent of the time, the meeting will be different from what you have imagined and prepared for.

   ii. Curveballs can be thrown at the start of a meeting, at the end, or anywhere in between.

   iii. Relevance wins, even if it's different from your game plan.

   iv. Leverage your preparation—including goals and roles, handoffs, SOS signals, and key messages—to manage unexpected events.

f. Client feedback: To ensure client relevance and to avoid in this high-pressure moment the natural reactions of mental rigidity and defensiveness:

   i. Seek out client feedback, from both live and virtual participants, at key transition and discussion points.

   ii. Leverage this information to refine important points.

   iii. Course-correct where needed. Neither of the two extremes—failing to ask or asking endlessly—is effective.

g. Key messages: To gain alignment as a team and with the client:

   i. Connect capabilities to client issues and outcomes.

   ii. Support one another in filling gaps left by a colleague.

h. Question and answer: To feel confident prior to closing:

   i. Budget at least 5–10 minutes for questions and answers.

   ii. Seek out lingering questions and concerns from stakeholders, including those who are participating virtually.

       iii. Leverage your team's work during Practice on handoffs, SOS signals, and key messages.

    i. Insights: To create new streams of dialogue and change thinking and perceptions through insights:

       i. Take advantage of the practice you've done.

       ii. Show patience and allow space for silence as customer stakeholders absorb and consider a new viewpoint.

    j. Closing: To clarify commitments and next steps:

       i. Budget at least five minutes to close.

       ii. Ask for the commitments you seek.

       iii. Lock down next steps.

       iv. End with enthusiasm, confidence, and appreciation, suitable to the meeting.

Figure 10.3 is a reminder of the tools available to help you and your selling squad get or stay in sync during Execute.

FIGURE 10.3 Execute Tools

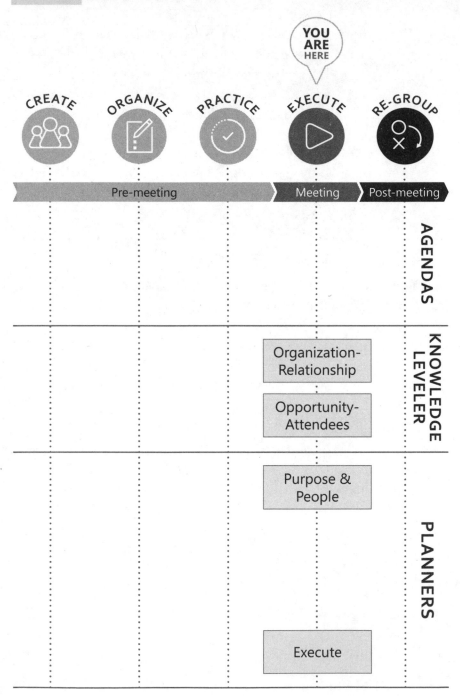

CHAPTER 10

NOTES TO SELF

1. Key points to remember about the Execute stage of the selling squad Build Process:

   a. _____

   b. _____

   c. _____

2. What actions will you take, and by when, to be effective during Execute, to:

   - Update your knowledge levelers? _____

   - Update your planners for:

     - Purpose and people _____

     - Team touchpoints—including team meet-up and re-group plans

       _____

     - Materials _____

     - Execute _____

   - Confirm on-site game plan for managing logistics, including rapport, seating plan, technology links, materials, etc.? _____

   - Stage a speedy warm-up review of key content and transitions?

     _____

3. To improve your long-term sales impact, you would like to:

   a. Stop: _____

   b. Start: _____

   c. Continue: _____

CHAPTER 11

RE-GROUP: COORDINATING FOLLOW-THROUGH AND GROWTH

FIGURE 11.1 Re-group Stage of a Selling Squad

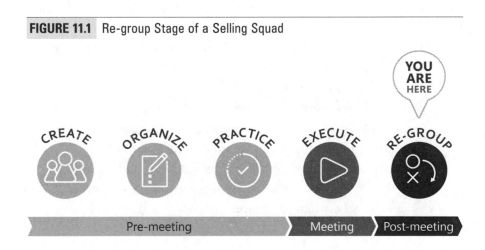

Imagine that your sales meeting just ended. What happens now . . . ?

The four teammates, introduced at the start of Chapter 10, left the customer's office feeling pretty good about the meeting. They walked out to the parking lot together and, before driving off, spent a few minutes going over the meeting. Bob apologized for being late, and the others assured him it was no issue. They all agreed the client was impressed, and that they made their key points. The account executive thanked them for making the time and promised to keep them posted as things developed. The group completed a round of vigorous handshakes, back-slaps, and high-fives before departing, as the customer, while on the phone, looked down from his window and wondered whether they all had just attended the same meeting.

Given the amount of preparation and energy that goes into a high-stakes client meeting, it's important to address what happens after the final handshakes.

Common Traps

I find that many teams are so engrossed in their preparation activities that they can miss the bigger picture. See if you recognize any of the following missteps that can occur following a sales meeting's completion:

- Celebrating, or commiserating, in the client's elevator or parking lot
- Not having a debrief meeting
- Believing that the conversation that takes place in the car or cab leaving the meeting is the same thing as a debrief
- Budgeting inadequate time to properly debrief
- One person taking responsibility for all follow-up
- Meeting of the mutual admiration society, with no purpose or agenda other than to reinforce positives and general impressions
- No feedback

Authors Jon Katzenbach and Douglas Smith talk about the importance of the feedback loop, gaining and incorporating feedback from outside the group that helps "advance the team toward achieving specific goals" and moving the team "closer to success." (Katzenbach & Smith, 2001, p. 105) Winning teams—orchestras, theater companies, Formula 1 racing teams, basketball teams, and, yes, selling teams—carry their rigor through to their follow-up activities.

Best Practices During Re-group

Here are some best practices to help you keep your team on path to win the business after the meeting has ended:

1. **Preschedule your Re-group meeting:** This reduces the risk that your colleagues will schedule that time for other purposes. This was part of your planning process for this meeting.

2. **Meet as soon as possible:** Research studies show that people forget as much as 73 percent of what they learned within two days of learning it. (Thalheimer, 2010, p. 30). Convene while the team's memories of the meeting exist in full color.

3. **Make attendance mandatory:** Regardless of organizational rank, the team's members are peers for the sales meeting they collaborated on. Each member's view on the meeting matters equally. Senior and junior, vocal and quiet, internal and external partner.

4. **Face it:** The best Re-group meetings happen face-to-face, and with meeting notes handy. Why? Your team just went through an intense experience together. This is an opportunity to acknowledge one another for the energy and work that you all put into your preparation and execution, and to share your take on what happened. A significant part of communication happens nonverbally. If you want to be sure to capture the full experience from your team, gather them together, as soon as possible following the meeting's end.

5. **Nearby:** Find a place such as a hotel lobby close to the customer meeting location where the team can breathe, focus, and properly debrief prior to launching off in different directions.

6. **Have a game plan:** Use a process that not only covers key subject areas, but also harnesses the group's collective intelligence by facilitating roughly equal contributions from each team member. Adopting this mind frame reminds you as the leader to prevent dominant voices from overpowering, and quiet voices from disappearing. Sandy Pentland, MIT professor and author

of *Social Physics*, attributes from his research 50 percent of group task performance to "diversity of ideas: everyone within a group contributing ideas and reactions, with similar levels of turn taking among the participants." (Pentland, 2014, p. 89) And, by all means, use the Re-group agenda here to manage that discussion.

During your Re-group meeting, there are several key areas that you will want to cover. (See Figure 11.2.)

- **Key learning points:** Bringing together multiple people from buying and selling organizations around a potential purchase decision happens every day and seems normal. It is also a much more complex event to understand than most pause to think about. Beyond the relationships among your team members, there are relationships among client stakeholders and between your team and theirs to consider. It is important to reflect on how these cross-perceptions changed during your sales meeting. Make sure that each team member gets an equal opportunity to share what he or she heard and saw during the meeting. This will give you as the selling squad leader multiple views on the same meeting, which gives you the best chance to incorporate these observations and arrive at a body of knowledge that is as close as possible to what happened within the space of the meeting.

- **Internal follow-up accountabilities:** Based on the team's observations and discoveries, lead a discussion that arrives at commitments to assume responsibility for the following:

  a. Who will take ownership for capturing key points agreed to by the team—collectively and individually?

  b. Leveraging extended team members and technology, where appropriate, who will enter meeting notes and follow-up information into your organization's customer relationship management system for easy reference in tracking progress?

  c. Who on the team will be responsible for delivering on each of the action items agreed to?

- **Client follow-up accountabilities:** Clarify accountability for follow-through with the client, including:

  a. Which team member will take the lead in following up with key client contacts?
  b. Remind those charged with client contact during follow-up to seek live touchpoints to continue momentum in building relationships (e-mail is a weak medium for dialogue).
  c. Gain client feedback on how well (or poorly) the meeting met their objectives. For significant sales presentations, some organizations conduct a formal post-mortem. It is conducted by someone outside the selling squad and at a senior enough level to convey the importance to the firm of the client's feedback. The goal is to make sure the client's feedback is captured fairly and objectively. Be sure that feedback is circulated among the team as appropriate so that the team can course-correct where needed and possible, and can continue to strengthen as a unit.
  d. Review and validate with the client the action plan, including accountabilities and timing for both organizations.
  e. If your team feels thank-you notes are appropriate, consider tasking individual team members with reaching out to their client counterparts, making sure that each stakeholder gets some level of contact.

- **Benchmark the meeting:** In many of the selling squad Re-group meetings that I observe or facilitate, teams wrestle with the question of whether the meeting was successful. This is especially tough to determine for meetings in which there is very little client engagement and dialogue. The simplest way to benchmark your meeting is to measure the outcome(s) versus your objective(s) going into the meeting. To do this, of course, means that your team went into the meeting with defined objectives.

FIGURE 11.2 Agenda 4: Re-group

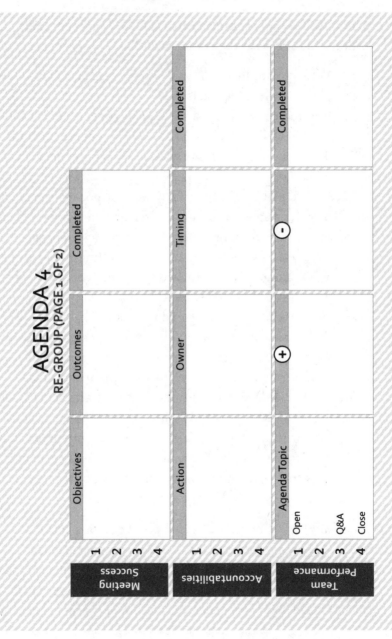

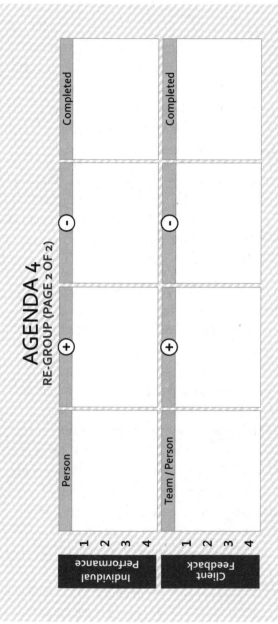

AGENDA 4
RE-GROUP (PAGE 2 OF 2)

Individual Performance	Person	+	–	Completed
1				
2				
3				
4				

Client Feedback	Team / Person	+	–	Completed
1				
2				
3				
4				

- **Assess the team's performance:** Reviewing teamwork high and low points will enable this group to strengthen their performance in the future. This is not individual feedback, yet. How did the team do throughout the presentation? Facilitate a discussion that invites each core group member to break down their feedback on the team's performance into pluses and minuses for each stage of the sales meeting or presentation. Guide team members to layer in how actual events played out relative to the group's plans and where there were examples of strong and weak teamwork. For example:

  > When we opened the meeting, we really seemed to impress the client stakeholder with the smoothness of our introductions and the relevance of our agenda. If I had to find a coaching point, we could have done a better job seeking their feedback on their agenda before rolling on.

- **Debrief individual team member performance:** This is the part of Re-group that is most often, in my experience, overlooked or intentionally avoided. I have coached selling squad leaders who crave feedback on how to lead their teams better. What they get after a meeting is "you were great" or "I can't think of anything you could have done differently." Feedback can feel uncomfortable for all involved. Handled poorly, it can damage professional relationships and friendships and hurt a person's confidence and self-esteem. Delivered well, your feedback has the potential to change someone's life, professionally and personally. It can also create the kind of trust with that person that will jump-start your team-building efforts when you next recruit him or her to one of your selling squads. What moments come to mind when you think of feedback delivered poorly and well?

  We have talked throughout the book about what feedback is and isn't, and why it's important. Because giving constructive peer-to-peer feedback is tough, here are some tips on delivering feedback effectively in more depth:

a. Gain agreement up front: Get agreement from each team member that they are willing to exchange feedback with you. This sets expectations and allows the team to be dialed in with one another throughout the meeting. This includes senior executives and subject matter experts. In my experience, the more senior and in demand someone is, the less real feedback they receive. Read another way, you have an opportunity to make a real impact on their contributions to your organization's sales efforts.

b. Schedule time for soon after the meeting: By all means, take time to think about what feedback you will share and how you will deliver it. This is especially true if you feel the feedback may be emotional for you to give, or for your colleague to receive, for example, if you felt someone torpedoed a sales meeting and ended your chance to compete for the business. Do aim to deliver your feedback as soon after the meeting as possible, but make sure you feel you are able to deliver it constructively.

c. Consider location: If the feedback is going to be substantive, honest, and well received, public places work poorly. Face-to-face is significantly better than phone, and e-mail is always a poor choice for feedback since the exchange does not happen in real time. Choose a location and time where the people involved will feel comfortable and focused.

d. One-on-one: It is rare that a team has built the level of trust and candor with one another that they are able to give and get substantive feedback in a group setting. For most teams, I recommend prescheduling one-on-one meetings, limiting time to 30 minutes. These pairings should be driven by the team based on trust and respect.

e. Start with yourself: In peer-to-peer feedback it is most effective to lead by example. Share your own views first on what you considered to be the things that worked well for you during the pitch, and those that you would do differently if you could hit the rewind button. Then invite your colleague to share his or her views on your high and low points. Then, switch. Have your colleague self-assess, before sharing your assessment.

f. Balanced: As discussed earlier, effective feedback is balanced. So, each person should come to the feedback discussion ready to share at least one strength and one area for improvement.

g. Specific: Feedback should be objective, not personal, and focused on specific language used or actions taken, or missed. This allows the recipient to replicate the hits and address the misses.

h. Honesty: Avoiding uncomfortable topics does not serve your teammate. Do consider how to share feedback so it is well received. Strike the balance we discussed earlier— brutal honesty and candy-coating are equally ineffective. Be direct and compassionate. For example:

> So, the client told you she just came into a large inheritance. I noticed that you smiled and said, "How wonderful!" You may have missed her sadness about this not being a great moment at all. My coaching point would be to express empathy at a moment like that and to ask a question about what happened. What's your reaction to that feedback?

i. Mutual: Feedback is best shared mutually between or among teammates. If you are going to give it, you must be willing to receive it as well. In their book, *Thanks for the Feedback,* Douglas Stone and Shelia Heen, lecturers at Harvard Law School, focused on how to best receive feedback. (Stone & Heen, 2014) Allow me to oversimplify their work into one key point: understand and don't judge feedback as you receive it. There's a tendency to allow those primitive survival, fight-or-flight instincts to take over causing you to deflect, defend, filter, and discard feedback that contrasts with your self-assessment. To take advantage of the opportunity to grow professionally, aim instead to understand the feedback, clarify as needed, take notes, and thank the giver. You decide what, if anything, to incorporate. But do make sure you and your teammate walk away from that moment feeling understood and supported—even if one or both of you disagree with the feedback.

Figure 11.3 is a recap of the tools available for an effective Re-group session.

Figure 11.4 is a roll-up of all the tools, segmented by each stage of the selling squad Build Process.

FIGURE 11.3 Re-group Tools

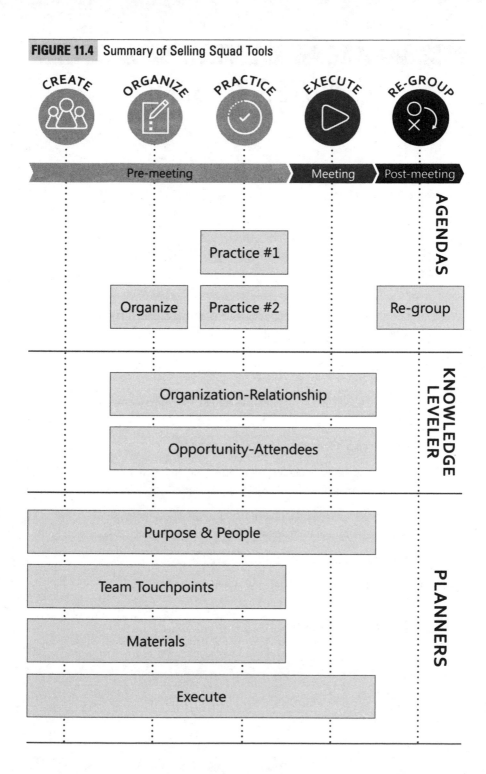

FIGURE 11.4 Summary of Selling Squad Tools

CREATE   ORGANIZE   PRACTICE   EXECUTE   RE-GROUP

Pre-meeting | Meeting | Post-meeting

AGENDAS

| | | Practice #1 | | |
| | Organize | Practice #2 | | Re-group |

KNOWLEDGE LEVELER

Organization-Relationship

Opportunity-Attendees

PLANNERS

Purpose & People

Team Touchpoints

Materials

Execute

CHAPTER 11

NOTES TO SELF

1. Key points to remember about the Re-group stage of the selling squad Build Process:

    a. _____

    b. _____

    c. _____

2. Opportunity you are working today with a selling squad that is in the Create, Organize, or Practice stage:

    _____

    What actions will you take, and by when, to plan an effective Re-group meeting, to:

    *   Update your agenda? _____

    *   Manage logistics, including meeting space and technology links for virtual participants? _____

    *   Gain closure on client follow-up accountabilities, meeting observations, and team feedback? _____

    *   Seek client feedback? _____

    *   Schedule one-on-one feedback sessions? _____

3. To improve your long-term sales impact, you would like to:

    a. Stop: _____

    b. Start: _____

    c. Continue: _____

PART III

CREATING A MORE COLLABORATIVE CLIMATE IN YOUR ORGANIZATION

CHAPTER 12

SPECIAL TIPS FOR AND ABOUT SENIOR EXECUTIVES ON SELLING SQUADS

Inviting a C-level executive to—or, if you're a senior executive, accepting an invite to participate in—a sales or client meeting can only be a huge positive, right?

Early in my sales career, I heard the CEO of my company say to us that he wanted to spend more time doing customer calls. So on those rare occasions when a prospect visited our headquarters, I looked for an opportunity to include him. When a prospect I had met at a conference called to tell me that he was going to be in town for other business, I thought, *This is my chance.* So I was thrilled to find out through the CEO's assistant that he was available and would be delighted to make the time. Locked and loaded. I diligently sent the CEO a memo (this is pre–e-mail!) with background information on the organization and person with whom we would be meeting. I was excited. So on the day of the meeting, my contact and I visited for a short time and then we headed up to the CEO's expansive office, which was filled with antiques. We took seats around a table in a sitting area. After some small talk, there was silence. The CEO looked at me, and I smiled and nodded back waiting for him to work his CEO magic. He began by asking questions about the client's organization and needs. As the meeting progressed, I grew anxious. He didn't talk about our organization as I had expected. When our end time arrived, he got up, thanked the client for coming, and mentioned that he hoped we would do business together at some point.

The meeting did not at all go as I had expected it to. On the positive side, the CEO's questions triggered responses that included new information. Alternatively, he hadn't delivered the company story the way I had hoped. Reflecting back on this, he was unclear about my expectations because I failed to convey them.

The Turbocharger

Turbocharger. Hear the word and you probably think robust power source. Competitive drivers and car manufacturers have used turbochargers for decades to boost engine power and race performance. In the hands of a skilled driver, this extra power can offer a competitive advantage. Putting that power, however, in the hands of someone less skilled or at the wrong time, can be fatal.

In the competitive world of selling, it is natural to seek a turbocharger-equivalent to boost performance in a sales meeting. At times this means a C-level executive—i.e., CEO, COO, CFO, CIO—agreeing to join a sales meeting or presentation. And why not? A C-level executive may be able to help advance a sale or retain a relationship, and in the process build the team leader's credibility with a client and even his or her colleagues.

Common Traps

However, it is a mistake to take this step lightly or impulsively, even with the most receptive and charismatic C-level executive. Their presence and contributions—no different from any other member of your selling squad—may prove to be an asset or liability. Some of the following mistakes made when including a senior-level executive in a sales pitch or client meeting may ring a bell or two:

- Believing that a C-level executive's title, presence, and personality can magically transform a poorly qualified opportunity or a poorly prepared team
- Treating him or her as untouchable, beyond coaching or preparation
- Banking on the fact that he or she automatically knows "what to do"
- Assuming that your deal carries the same importance to him or her as it does to you
- Relying on the status that executive brings and not bringing your own A-game as a result

In the preceding scenario, I fell into each one of these traps. Well, I did bring my A-game, which at the time hardly deserved an A.

Impact of a Senior Executive on a Selling Squad

Without guidance, what did my CEO do? He led, of course. He took control of the meeting, and, in that case, he needed to because there was no other team leader present in the room.

Leaders lead. And so the lesson from this story and common mistakes is that, without your effective team leadership, a C-level executive may take control of the meeting, moving you away from an otherwise winning game plan and hurting your credibility with the client. A senior leader playing a minor role can be equally hurtful. What does that convey about your C-level executive? Your organization? The profit margin in your proposal? You?

Whether you are the senior executive or the team leader who asked that leader to join you on a sales call or pitch, it's important to be aware of how this addition changes the group's dynamics.

As Dr. Heidi Gardner points out in her *Harvard Business Review* article "Coming Through When It Matters Most," colleagues working together in important moments breeds what she calls "the performance pressure paradox." (Gardner, *HBR*, April 2012, p. 83) Based on her research with cross-specialty work teams in professional services firms, as pressure rises people tend to fall back into their hierarchal roles in the organization.

Since the C-level executive's role supersedes all others on your team, he or she will effectively take over as the team's leader when the pressure rises—i.e., as the meeting approaches. And while your CFO, for instance, may be incredibly talented and polished, and have an impressive knowledge of the financial markets, the other team members are likely to be far more plugged into what drives the client contacts on this opportunity. No matter, deferring authority to your CFO in this case overweights the CFO's experience and knowledge and underweights the input from other team members who possess significant client knowledge. While being smart is important, to win a sales meeting your selling squad needs to be relevant. Your team, including the CFO, needs to be aware of these natural dynamics and manage the team's interactions, particularly in high-pressure moments, in order to make sure the team stays on its path to accomplish its performance goal.

Best Practices for Senior Executives on a Selling Squad

C-level executives can be a great asset and turbocharge your selling squad's efforts to create a winning sales meeting. Here are five rules of engagement for a C-level executive participating in an effective sales call, pitch, or client meeting:

1. Ask

Obvious, yes? Less obvious is what it takes to prepare for that ask so that it results in an enthusiastic "yes."

- **Selling squad leader tip:** Decide and convey to the executive why participating in this effort aligns with his or her goals, how it will help the client, and what is the expected impact on the sales effort.
- **Senior executive tip:** Choose carefully the sales opportunities on which you participate. Resist the impulse to give an immediate reply. Jumping onto a losing cause only increases your firm's

loss on a pursuit. At a minimum, the salesperson's request for you to participate is a great opportunity to reinforce the importance of qualifying opportunities. In an earlier chapter, we discussed how selling squad leaders can qualify opportunities using four questions—ensuring there is sufficient reason for the client to change and work with your organization now, and for your firm to work with them. Listening to your salesperson's rationale for pursuing this deal should make it clear whether this is a "Hail Mary" pass or a well-thought-out move that could win the deal. Your participation at the right times in the pursuit of qualified opportunities can be a game-changer.

2. Define and Communicate Expectations

This should include clearly conveying:

1. Goals and roles for the meeting, including who will be the selling squad's leader
2. Expectations for participation in preparing for and debriefing the meeting with the team
3. Defining how, when, and where to give and get feedback

This is an opportunity to strengthen your selling partnership should you work together again on a future opportunity.

3. Prepare Together

C-level executives should attend team prep sessions, with your understanding of the possibility of more pressing conflicts.

- **Selling squad leader tip:** When the executive is able to be there, be efficient:
    1. Transfer essential knowledge given your leader's role in the sales meeting.
    2. Run through the opening, including your leader's welcome message and introduction.

3. Review whatever additional topics, such as a company overview, your leader will address in the meeting.
4. Be clear on your role as team leader, including who will close and how that will be done.

■ **Senior executive tip:** Resist the impulse to take over because the team will follow you if you lead. Seek to understand and be the intricately jigsawed piece the team needs to complete their puzzle. Also, humor and off-the-cuff remarks have their time and place. Have you ever heard a fellow executive introduce himself and refer to his role as "Overhead"? What can be funny in an internal meeting, where the audience reports to you, can be disastrous in a sales meeting. Preparing together reduces the chance of a negative surprise.

4. Set Intra-meeting Ground Rules

The senior executive should take a seat that appropriately conveys his or her role in your organization, and lines up with the customer's senior-most decision maker.

■ **Selling squad leader tip:** Once the meeting gets started, stay engaged and provide cues and handoffs to your teammates, including the executive, as appropriate.
■ **Senior executive tip:** Seek a seat that allows you to make full eye contact with their senior contact, without sitting directly opposed in the "locking horns" position, or to their right, which allows sidebars. Also, it can feel odd shifting into an environment where the authority, pace, and scope is being set by others. To support the team in its winning game plan, be sure to take your cues from the team leader, keeping improvisation to a minimum.

5. Debrief Together

There are a number of follow-up activities that should be considered: thank-you notes and feedback among them.

- **Selling squad leader tip:** Consider drafting a thank-you note on the team's behalf for your C-level executive to sign. Ask for feedback on your role as team leader and on other team members. Consider collecting and distilling the team's feedback—both pluses and minuses —and deliver the key points when you are one-on-one with him or her. Also, be sure to acknowledge your C-level executive's time in preparing for, attending and contributing to the meeting. Ask how he or she would like to stay apprised of future developments.

- **Senior executive tip:** You can play an important role in reviewing the team's high and low points during the meeting. Providing individual feedback should be handled carefully. Be aware that your feedback to team members takes on extra gravity. To strengthen your impact in future sales meetings, consider accepting feedback from at least the team leader. If your experience is like mine was as a former leader and that of many C-level executives I coach, you may get very little objective feedback. This is a shame since you play such an important role in sales meetings. Your own development as a member of selling squads will strengthen your power to advance and close deals at pivotal points.

Including a C-level executive in a sales meeting can be both an exciting and intimidating move in a broader sales or client retention strategy. Such an executive's presence alone is rarely the "magic bullet" expected and needed. In the right opportunity, setting, and timing, however, executives can play a significant role in winning a new client or retaining an existing one.

Keep the five tips above in mind for upcoming sales meetings. A C-level executive, properly positioned, can turbocharge a selling team's sales efforts to give it the extra boost needed to motor into the winner's circle.

CHAPTER 12

NOTES TO SELF

1. Key points to remember about including or being a senior executive on a selling squad:

   a. _____

   b. _____

   c. _____

2. Opportunity you are working today that will include you or someone else as the team's senior executive:

   _____

   What actions will you take, and by when, to plan an effective contribution:

   - During Organize? _____
   - During Practice? _____
   - During Execute? _____
   - During Re-group? _____

3. To improve your long-term sales impact, you would like to:

   a. Stop: _____

   b. Start: _____

   c. Continue: _____

CHAPTER 13

SPECIAL TIPS FOR AND ABOUT SUBJECT MATTER EXPERTS ON SELLING SQUADS

Imagine you are an 18-year-old college basketball player and, despite limited playing time during the regular season, you are pulled off the bench and put into the national championship game, with 13 minutes left on the clock and your team down by nine points. If you're Duke University's Grayson Allen playing the final game for the 2015 NCAA Men's Basketball Championship in his freshman year, you steal the ball from your opponent (who happens to be the national player of the year), sink a three-point shot, and get fouled, hitting both of your free throws. All in the space of 70 seconds. And in the process, you change the game's momentum and turn a sure loss into a national championship.

In business-to-business selling, subject matter experts (SMEs) come off the bench to play an increasingly important role in high-stakes sales meetings. However selling is something SMEs may do infrequently, so the salesperson faces a question similar to the one that Duke's coach confronted as he eyed Grayson Allen: Will my SME be ready when I need him?

In an earlier chapter we addressed how to best leverage a C-level executive in a customer meeting. Here we address a related topic: how to leverage an SME for maximum impact in an effective sales meeting.

Examples of SMEs

Subject matter experts work in a wide range of roles across various industries. Examples include:

- In technology, a systems engineer, solutions architect, or applications specialist
- In professional services, a practice leader or specialist
- In wealth management, a tax, estates, or fiduciary specialist
- In investment management, a quantitative portfolio manager, operations, or compliance officer

Just as Duke's coach Mike Krzyzewski's call was calculated and informed, so should your decision in recruiting even the most receptive and articulate SME to your selling squad. Their presence and contributions—no different from any other member of your selling team—could prove to be an asset or liability.

Common SME Traps

See which of these common mistakes you recognize from when salespeople include an SME in a sales pitch or client meeting:

- Assuming that the SME's expertise and credentials can overcome a weak opportunity or an unprepared team
- Giving the SME diva treatment and no proper preparation
- Assuming the expert knows "what to do"
- Believing the SME cares about winning the presentation as much as you do
- Allowing an SME to operate as if the meeting's goal is to impress the client with their qualifications and knowledge
- Demonstrating none of your own credibility

Without guidance, experts are likely to do what they do: demonstrate their subject matter expertise. They may take control of the discussion, going deep into an issue that takes you away from an otherwise winning game plan and hurting your credibility with the client. An SME playing a minor role can be equally damaging. What does that convey about your SME? Your organization? The profit margin you built into the proposal?

In Chapter 12, I referenced Dr. Heidi Gardner's work with professional services firms and what she describes as "the performance pressure paradox." (Gardner, *HBR*, 2012, p. 83) (One of the other effects that she discovered in work teams as pressure rose was a tendency to move to approaches that reduced risk to the individuals on the team. For a team that has asked a brilliant technologist to join them on a customer meeting, this might mean a move away from a more creative approach that has not yet been tried by your organization and opting instead for an approach everyone feels comfortable with because it has worked in the past. If the tried-and-true approach for your organization does not line up with client's needs, you can see how risk avoidant behavior can happen, can feel right, and can produce a losing outcome.

Best Practices for SMEs on Selling Squads

Subject matter experts can be a game-changer in a selling squad's efforts to create a winning sales meeting. Here are five tips for properly leveraging an SME in an effective sales call, pitch, or client meeting:

1. **Choose carefully:** Technical expertise is a given. Just as a selling squad leader should choose an SME carefully, SMEs should also choose which teams and opportunities are best suited for them.

   ▪ **Selling squad leader tip:** Think through how an SME's delivery style will mesh with those of the client stakeholders. What will he or she be like as a collaborator in your preparation and presentation? As with a senior executive, prepare for the ask so it results in a yes by conveying how participating in this effort lines up with your SME's goals, the value it will bring to the client, and the expected outcome on the pitch.

- **SME tip:** Selling may not be your focus and may even be something you loath doing. Choose wisely to be sure you are investing time where you see a payoff. Do ask the salesperson why this opportunity is so exciting, look for reasons that are more substantive than a dollar amount, and see how this experience will benefit you and your practice area. Say yes if you are willing to be an engaged member of the team. And if the answer is no, please offer more than "I'm busy." Be direct and include your rationale so the team leader can learn how better to leverage your talents.

2. **Define and communicate your expectations:** For both the selling squad leader and the SME. this should include a mutual understanding of:

   a. Meeting goals
   b. Roles in the meeting, and who is the team's leader
   c. Expectations for participation in preparing for and debriefing the meeting

3. **Prepare together:** The SME, now a member of the selling squad, has a role to play in preparing for an effective sales meeting or presentation.

   - **Selling squad leader tips:**

     a. Give your SME the need-to-knows from the team's knowledge leveler about the client organization, stakeholder roles, the relationship, the opportunity, and so on.
     b. Insist on practicing the opening, including introductions, so you can hear and coach the SME as to content and timing.
     c. Ask the SME to run through the key topics you have asked him or her to address in the customer meeting, so that you and the team can provide feedback to better resonate with the client and stay within the meeting's time boundaries.
     d. Define the SME's role, from open to close, including when the SME does not have a primary speaking role.

- **SME tips:**

  a. Realize that a sales meeting is not a test of your experience and expertise. Rather, success will be determined by how well you fit your capabilities to what the customer is trying to accomplish.

  b. Request to be briefed so you understand the opportunity, meeting dynamics, and value you are expected to bring to facilitate the client's decision and to advance the sales process.

  c. Budget your time, not just for reading through briefing materials or attending a launch meeting, but to join the team for practice calls or meetings and for a debrief.

  d. Bring an openness to how best you can accomplish the client's and team's objectives. This will likely include getting feedback and describing your experience and capabilities in a way that is different from, and more client-specific than, the way you usually explain them.

  e. Be prepared to fully engage during the customer meeting, even when the conversation moves to topics that fall outside your area of expertise. Demonstrate your interest in your colleagues and the client, by staying alert and making eye contact with those who are speaking.

  Preparing together increases the odds of delivering on each other's expectations and achieving the goal.

4. **Set intra-meeting ground rules:** Sales meetings can feel like foreign terrain for an SME. In internal meetings, he or she is the expert and center of attention. This is not so in sales meetings where the selling squad's leader is a salesperson—who may fall below the SME on an organizational chart—and where the focus is on, and the cadence is set by, the client. This is especially important when questions arise—whether in a formal Q&A section of your presentation or on the fly. What may be a simple question asked out of curiosity by one client contact may look to the SME like a can't-miss opportunity to show his or her domain expertise.

- **Selling squad leader tip:** Aim for a seating plan that aligns the SME with his or her client counterpart.
- **SME tip:** Remember that your expertise may have helped get the meeting; what produces a winning outcome is relevance. And relevance is proven by linking your deep subject matter knowledge to your team's deep customer knowledge. To make sure that you stay on point, take your cues from the team leader, keeping improvisation to a minimum. Stick to the team's game plan of how questions will be fielded, clarified, allocated to and answered by team members, and squared back with the questioner. If you have ideas that conflict with the team's game plan, be sure to raise them with the team prior to the meeting so they can be discussed, debated, and, where appropriate, incorporated into the team's collective game plan. This may seem obvious, but taking time during a client meeting to prove that you're right about a point that was dismissed as insignificant during the team's preparation sessions will hurt the credibility of your organization, your team, and you. It will bring any momentum that had been built in a sales meeting to a screeching stop, and it will most likely cause your team to lose the business or the opportunity to advance the sale. The one exception is if you are in sync with the team leader, and that leader cues you with the SOS signal to go with your idea for Plan B that was discussed in advance.

5. **Debrief together.** An SME can play an important role in reviewing the team's high and low points during the meeting. Exchanging feedback can strengthen future meetings and pitches.

   - **Selling squad leader tip:** Be sure to acknowledge the SME's time in preparing for and taking the meeting, and thank the SME for his or her contributions. Be ready to share feedback that is balanced, specific, and honest. Ask how the SME would like to stay apprised of future developments with your sales opportunity.

- **SME tip:** Come to this conversation prepared both to receive feedback on your contributions to the effort, and to provide feedback to your colleague that is equally balanced, specific, and honest. Avoid judging the feedback as it is being shared. Clarify, record, and thank any attempts to help you grow professionally.

An SME's participation in a sales meeting can help advance a client relationship and even close a deal. On its own, however, an SME's involvement will not somehow fill gaping holes in a sales or client retention strategy. In the right setting and with attentive coaching, an SME can successfully create new streams of dialogue, change perceptions about your firm if needed, and build confidence among stakeholders to make a commitment to your organization.

Leverage these five tips in preparing for your next team sales meeting or pitch. An SME's ability to jump off the bench to give his or her selling squad the extra boost needed to convert this opportunity into a win just might be the game-changer in the selling squad's efforts.

CHAPTER 13

NOTES TO SELF

1. Key points to remember about including or being a SME on a selling squad:

   a. _____

   b. _____

   c. _____

2. Opportunity you are working today that will include you or someone else as the team's SME:

   _____

   What actions will you take, and by when, to plan an effective contribution?

   - During Organize? _____
   - During Practice? _____
   - During Execute? _____
   - During Re-group? _____

3. To improve your long-term sales impact, you would like to:

   a. Stop: _____

   b. Start: _____

   c. Continue: _____

HITTING THE "ICE" BUTTON

There will be times when an interesting opportunity or meeting crests quickly and there is precious little time between when you get the call and when you need to show up at the client's site with a selling squad.

Because you are now doing more focused work on qualifying opportunities, you most likely are more comfortable with prioritizing and preparing for your best opportunities. However, there is less time to devote to low-priority prospects.

Still, you will take such meetings for various reasons and you will find that there simply isn't the time to prepare the way you would for a top-shelf, qualified opportunity, even though there will be multiple players on your team and the client's side of the table. You understand that your team's chances of getting in sync as an effective selling squad, in the limited time available, are exceedingly low.

Common Traps

When time is short, you may end up making some of these mistakes:

- Use a cookie-cutter approach to similar meetings in the past: same people, materials, and agenda. Whatever, let's do it.

- Wing it. Most sales professionals and those who participate frequently in sales meetings consider themselves quick on their feet. This confidence is multiplied when you have a group of colleagues who work together often, know each other well, and have a successful track record.
- Share minimal communication in advance of the meeting. Knowledge transfer may be accomplished through a single e-mail that combines meeting details plus background information on the buying organization and sales opportunity.

Best Practices for Hitting the "ICE" Button

Hitting the ICE ("in case of emergency") button is reserved for those cases when you're short on time and unable to prepare to sell like a team as we have discussed up to this point. I want to be super-clear here: hitting the ICE button will not win a high-stakes opportunity against strong competition. This will, however, allow you and your colleagues to progress from feeling totally unprepared to somewhat prepared. I feel confident that if being "somewhat prepared" is what you are aiming for in your sales meetings, you wouldn't have purchased or read this far in this book. So I offer the following comments as not a cure-all, but as a last-minute cure-a-little.

I have found that once teams begin using the process described in this book for their qualified and important sales meetings, they are less willing to take meetings they cannot be fully prepared for and ones that take them away from better opportunities. When you consider hitting the ICE button, either by choice or out of necessity, narrow your prep activities to the five following items, each of which you will recognize from earlier in the book:

1. **Knowledge leveling:** Focus your team's attention on what the client or prospect is trying to accomplish, and why. Use the four questions to determine whether a qualified opportunity exists. Whatever you are unable to answer will form your priority

questions for the meeting. Assuming you decide to pursue an opportunity with this customer, you can figure out where this opportunity, the people with whom you are meeting, and your company's past work fit into the customer organization.

2. **Roles and goals:** When time is short, I find that selling teams often fall back into their organizational roles. Someone on the selling squad must take the lead. If there is no clear choice, select as your leader the person with the most client knowledge or at least the skills to manage the team and the meeting. Also define how the others on the team will support the leader. As for goals, see if you can agree on what you can realistically walk away from this meeting with—a verbal or written agreement, a recommendation to the board, a follow-up meeting including others within the next three weeks. Walking in with a clear goal—as imperfect as it might be—around which the team is unified has a magical way of creating shared intent and focus. Even when you and your team are not as prepared as you'd like to be.

3. **Opening:** Sort out how introductions will be handled and in what sequence. It takes only a few minutes to run through this a few times in the car on the way to the meeting. Getting this right gives your team an early win and builds team confidence and momentum.

4. **Agenda/responsibilities:** Break down the meeting into a few simple parts. This allows the client to keep track with you, and also enables the team to keep the discussion on track. Here is a generic example that can work:

> We're planning on covering three topics today: (1) make sure we understand all the dimensions of your request, (2) share some initial ideas and experiences related to the topic, and (3) define next steps around where your needs and our abilities overlap. How does that sound as a game plan for today's discussion?

> Think: (1) needs, (2) ideas, (3) action plan. Stay focused as a team. For each topic, be clear on who owns it. For last-minute

meetings, I find it best to minimize the number of handoffs. My default recommendation is that the team leader takes primary responsibility for all topics and signals team members in and out within each topic. This is easier to visualize and manage without preparation.

5. **The close:** The team leader will typically close—but work out how. This can be done in about a minute and can make the difference between leaving the meeting with an order or a handful of air. If you are the leader, practice your ask until it feels natural and on point with your meeting goal.

Two Final Tips on Last-Minute Preparation

There are two points worth adding to the short-cut tips mentioned above. First, materials don't win or lose opportunities; teams do. So, when time is short, don't waste time on customizing a presentation. Use a standard or recent presentation. That said, if you're bringing materials, each team member should choose and know where to find one "power page" that illustrates a process, design, or structure, for example, and from which a team member's comments can be launched.

Second, SOS signals, like the word *bluebird*, are effective when the team has time to practice with it. When this is not possible, insist upon a no-improvisation rule. Rather, when a team member picks up on something, commit to the process of posing questions to one other to maintain your ability to adapt during the meeting. For example, your product specialist picks up a cue that the client stakeholder's goals are different from what you assumed. Here is an example of how that specialist might signal that to the team leader: "Tim, it seems as if XYZ Associates is more focused on driving growth in a new channel. How would that change your reply to that question?"

In summary, these five steps will not transform a losing effort. They may, however, keep your chances alive, allow you to qualify the opportunity, and enter the meeting room more prepared than three strangers who wandered in off the street.

CHAPTER 14

NOTES TO SELF

1. Key points to remember about hitting the "ICE" button:

   a. _____

   b. _____

   c. _____

2. Opportunity you are working today that will probably require you to hit the "ICE" button:

   _____

3. What actions will you take, and by when, to:

   • Possibly avoid parking lot preparation? _____

   • Plan your parking lot prep, if required? _____

   • Coordinate a Re-group call or meeting? _____

   • To improve your long-term sales impact, you would like to:

   a. Stop: _____

   b. Start: _____

   c. Continue: _____

SPECIAL TIPS ON CO-SELLING WITH AFFILIATES AND PARTNERS

In many channels, salespeople and other customer-facing professionals go to market with people outside their own organization. These can include technology partners, affiliates, and consultants. The person with whom you may be co-selling represents an affiliate or third-party partner company that fills a gap in your firm's product, solution, or service offering. So how does co-selling with a third party affect your efforts to put together a winning selling squad?

The short answer: Unless you have worked together before, it will probably make it tougher. Why? Well, recall all that's involved in building a group, transforming them into a team, and then preparing for, executing on, and following up from an effective client or prospect meeting. We've talked already about how tough it is to gain trust and work effectively with people outside your own little slice of the organization. Working with external partners is even more extreme, when you consider the differences in corporate culture, philosophies, goals, skill level, sales process, willingness, and/or ability to commit time to fully get in sync with your team.

Creating a Team with External Partners

The first question you face with external partners or affiliates is whether they should be part of the selling squad's core or extended team. Go through the same assessment you would with an internal colleague to determine whether their presence at the meeting is necessary and material. If not, is it possible that they could contribute to your core team's efforts by supplying information, insights, and materials? Perhaps this would allow someone on your team to explain that partner's capabilities and how that partner would be integrated into your overall offer.

Leveraging the Tools

Let's say you've decided that someone from that partner or affiliate company needs to be part of the meeting and, as a result, part of your core team. Since that person will be part of your selling squad, how would you adapt the process for knowledge leveling, planning, and practice you do with internal partners?

- **Knowledge leveling:** It is fair to question just how much knowledge leveling you can or should do with someone outside your organization, someone who might at some point be a competitor, someone who may not be covered under any nondisclosure agreements your organization has executed. If you want them to make the desired impact on the meeting, however, that person needs to come prepared. That person doesn't need to see all your account planning work, just what is essential for him or her to play the desired role. And be careful to not overshare information your organization has worked hard to gain.

    Information on the buying organization and opportunity will help the person. You might consider holding back your responses to the four qualifying questions and past relationships.
- **Planning:** You will recall you now have planners to help you coordinate people, materials, and team touchpoints. Your

external partners should certainly know who else will be on your team. They can and should also play a part in your team's discussion on what materials, including presentation pages and agreements, should be developed. And they should be included in team touchpoints so their presence and comments can be aligned with the group's through the preparation, execution, and follow-up stages of the process. Depending on the nature of your relationship with this partner or affiliate, you may want to hold back sharing information on the customer stakeholders, where they fit into their organization, and how they figure into the decision-making body.

- **Practice:** Your partner should be included in all practices—including Organize, Practice, and Re-group meetings—if your goal is for them to be seen by the customer as a cohesive part of your team and offer. You might consider carving out an insiders-only part of your team touchpoints, so that you can (1) coach the other team members on what should and shouldn't be shared with your external partner and (2) share information among each other without constraints.

External partners may fill a gap that would otherwise prevent you from competing for the business. That's the upside. What's required to capture this upside is the added time and effort it may take you to ensure their contributions help you win the pitch, while making certain that you stay in control of the opportunity.

CHAPTER 15

NOTES TO SELF

1. Key points to remember about including affiliates or external partners on a selling squad:

   a. _____

   b. _____

   c. _____

2. Opportunity you are currently working with affiliates or external partners:

   _____

3. Who will represent that/those organization(s)? _____

4. What actions will you take, and by when, to plan their effective contributions?

   a. During Organize? _____

   b. During Practice? _____

   c. During Execute? _____

   d. During Re-group? _____

5. To improve your long-term sales impact, you would like to:

   a. Stop: _____

   b. Start: _____

   c. Continue: _____

SELLING SQUADS AND PRICE NEGOTIATIONS

There are many excellent books on negotiating, including some that cover the complexity of managing multiparty negotiations. Rather than covering the topic deeply here, what is important to think through in the context of effective team selling is the question of how to properly address pricing issues in a group sales or customer meeting.

Common Traps

There are several mistakes that selling squads commonly make in price negotiations. Which ones seem familiar to you?

1. **They don't realize they are negotiating:** In the course of a sales meeting, one of the customer stakeholders asks a question about price or terms. When teams sell, they tend to do a lot of finding and pleasing. So, when a customer asks a question about service guarantees, someone on the team replies, "Absolutely, we can do that!" And for a question on whether your firm offers discounts, someone feels comfortable remarking, "Our fees take into account the relationship." As good-hearted as those instincts are, they are misplaced at such moments. Increasingly account executives and sales teams field pricing-related

comments and questions from very sharp negotiators, including procurement officers, senior-level finance executives, and private equity sponsors. They know how to negotiate and know when the counterparty doesn't. They take advantage of this mismatch, usually for their gain and the seller's loss. Casual comments from the selling team convey to the other party that you will cave—both on guarantees and discounts.

2. **They don't prepare for it:** Negotiating well is tough enough when it is done between two people. Adding bodies, voices, and perceptions on both client and seller sides of the table makes it way more complex to manage effectively. Even a well-prepared sales executive can be undone, as in the previous situation, by an overeager colleague who has not been properly prepared for what may appear to be an insignificant or uncomfortable moment. Skilled negotiators have an uncanny ability to find the weakest link, and on your selling squad there may be more than one.

3. **They respond to tactics:** As a salesperson, you probably like the notion of win-win negotiating outcomes. However, you may find that many of your client counterparts are just fine with win-lose outcomes when negotiating price and terms with you. Among the gems that you may have seen buyers use are:

   - Making ultimatums, such as take it or leave it positions
   - Using emotional traps such as mock outrage
   - Bringing up past mistakes your firm made
   - Appealing to your sense of fairness, reminding you about how much work they have given you in the past
   - Making empty promises, as in "We'll take care of you down the road"
   - Using silence
   - Walking away from the bargaining table

   If as an experienced salesperson these sorts of tactics make you uncomfortable, how would you imagine your fellow selling squad members—senior executive, subject matter expert, technician, junior colleague—feel at those moments? How will they respond?

These tactics are designed to make you and team members feel replaceable, commodified, and desperate for the agreement on any terms. Customers use them because they often work.

4. **They get defensive:** The procurement officer, for example, before you even begin your opening comments, flips to the part of your book that contains the fee proposal, whistles, smiles at her colleagues, and states, "Wow, these fees are way high." Even more so in front of your own colleagues, it can feel as though you and your organization are being attacked. Your body, in response, goes into survival mode and triggers a fight-or-flight reaction—in this case fight. Your team's response may be to defend why you structured the fees the way you did, how competitive they are in the market, and how great your firm is. Perhaps your senior-level executive also jumps in to defend the fee levels. Despite all the factual information in the world, what gets transmitted to the other side of the table is desperation, weakness, and digging into a set position on price. Beyond that, this curveball succeeds in throws you and your team off-balance, off your agenda, and away from your game plan for the meeting.

5. **They avoid the topic:** Here is the other side of that fight-or-flight impulse. In this case, you or someone on your team replies that fees are important but so is value; you then shift to that part of your presentation where you feel you show the strongest value. You and your team are human and it may feel natural to respond to the instinct to go into flight mode. When price discussions are left unaddressed, rest assured, they will return.

6. **They feel no leverage:** When you sell into a very competitive market and, when a prospect is sizeable and attractive, it can feel as though the client has all the cards and you have none. Discussing price and terms at such moments put you and your team in a position where you can only win by giving up things and heading for a lose-win outcome.

7. **They feel compelled to fill the silence:** Experienced negotiators often choose to use silence at the negotiating table because it makes talkers and pleasers—including many salespeople—and inexperienced presenters want to reduce the tension in the moment. This signals weakness and gives an information advantage to your counterpart.

The Complexity of a Group Negotiation

During a sales meeting, selling squads can find themselves in the middle of a group negotiation. There may be disagreements within the buying team about certain issues, and there could be rifts within your own selling squad on certain points. Negotiating skillfully is an advanced selling skill. Negotiating effectively with a group of buyers, as a team of sellers, is significantly more complex. Max Bazerman and Margaret Neale in their book, *Negotiating Rationally*, state it well:

> The dynamics of group negotiation are far more complex than those of two-party negotiations. With two parties, there are two sets of interests and one interaction. With three parties, the network grows to three sets of individual interests, three possible interactions between any two players, and one interaction of all three. . . . This web of interests and relationships become increasingly complex as the numbers grow. (Bazerman & Neale, 1992, p. 128)

Best Practices for Negotiating in a Group Sales Meeting

Here are some reminders for how you and your team can feel prepared for those moments where price pressure is applied:

- **Know when you're negotiating:** This goes for both you and your team. As Linda Richardson put it in her classic sales book,

Stop Telling, Start Selling, "any time you are discussing price or terms, you have crossed the fine line between selling and negotiating." (Richardson, 1998, p. 83)

- **Know your process:** There are many effective processes on the topic of negotiations. When a price objection or demand gets put on the table by a customer, you should first, know how you are going to acknowledge it, think about the questions you're going to ask to better understand what's behind the comment or demand, before finally attempting to resolve it.

  For example, let's say that a customer demands, "I need this done by Friday!" A novice selling squad may look at each other and, in the heat of the moment, agree to this demand which is going to be nearly impossible to deliver.

  Consider an alternative to the same demand:

  Acknowledge: "It seems like there's some urgency."

  Question: "What's driving this?"

  In response, let's imagine that the customer's response is: "We're getting a lot of heat from senior management on this."

  Respond: "It sounds like the urgency is being driven by all the visibility around this project. We proposed a delivery date of one week from Wednesday, to ensure a seamless installation with zero errors or drama—especially important given senior management's focus on this." (Silence)

  This exchange demonstrates confidence, positions you to gain information, and enables you to emphasize preparation and value.

- **Prepare individually:** Experienced salespeople know, or should know, that among the things they need to sort through in advance of a mutual-gains negotiation are: the issues on the table; the interests of each party (meaning what are the parties trying to accomplish, not what they are demanding); the alternatives available to each party to meet their interests; and the criteria against which both parties can determine that they are getting what they need from an agreement. They know to also consider what commitments and relationship outcomes they are seeking. With multiple stakeholders, the job is tougher as each customer stakeholder is likely to vary in its interests.

- **Prepare as a group:** Part of your go-time preparation should include discussing who on your team will handle pricing-related questions, and what other team members should be doing at that time. If for your Practice session, you have recruited someone from outside the pitch team to role-play the client, this would be a great opportunity for them to help you practice your response.

- **Practice silence:** Now we're not talking about lighting incense and staging a séance. The tactic of silence can also be used by your selling squad. Remember how the example in the "Know your process" paragraph above ended with silence? It's critical at high-stakes moments—such as those where profit margin is created or lost—that you and your team have sorted out roles. This includes who will take the lead in discussing price and, importantly, what everyone else will be doing at that time. Even if that thing that everyone else is doing is . . . not talking. There's an old adage in negotiating that "he who talks first loses." Practice this a few times so that your colleagues with less experience at the negotiating table get comfortable with resisting their big-hearted instincts to fill the silence and, instead, contribute to the success of a well-planned moment.

- **Gain alignment as a selling team:** Everyone, including those on your team, has interests which may diverge from your own. You can imagine how a member of your team who wants the business and feels strongly that your firm's fees are expensive may, in the actual client meeting, signal through his or her language or body language that there is room to move. Resolving differences, again, does not mean gaining consensus. Decision rights should go to the people who are in the best position to make the call. It's important that everyone has a chance to be fully heard before decision making and that everyone understands and is aligned with the approach that the team will take during the meeting, even if a team member disagrees. There should be no surprises among the selling squad when discussing price or terms with a customer.

- **Understand group dynamics:** It is easy in high-stakes moments to view the client side of the table as a monolith, fully aligned in its interests. In reality, there are likely to be all sorts of different views and relationships among them—only a fraction of which you can see. Understand also that, when someone on their side pushes on price, it may have more to do with advancing an internal agenda among colleagues than it has to do with your proposal's appeal. Recognize in those moments that by acknowledging and listening to, rather than battling, that stakeholder in the group setting, you allow that person to advance his or her internal agenda and save face among colleagues, without making any commitments on the spot.

- **Avoid seeking agreements in a group setting:** The simplest way to "get to yes" is to leverage sales meetings to gain and give information that will help the client make a vendor choice, and the seller to qualify the opportunity. Exploring needs behind demands and testing your value proposition are ways to put you in a better position to negotiate fees when you are ready. Know the roles of the client stakeholders and, where possible, seek agreement to negotiate price and terms in a separate, one-on-one meeting.

- **Show your value:** A favorite line among professional services firms is "We bring a lot of value." If you're willing to take a step back from that familiar phrase, it's hard to get away from the fact that this conveys nothing. Value is defined in terms that are meaningful to client stakeholders. Assuming your selling efforts have been focused on gaining an information advantage over your competitors, this is the time to link the components of your proposal to customer needs. The stronger the perceived value to the client of what you bring, the more pricing leverage you have and, in turn, the more confident you will feel at these moments. Selling squad members can help draw those links, directing their comments to their closest counterpart and leveraging their understanding of that stakeholder's challenges.

- **Know your "BATNA":** Those familiar with the seminal negotiating book, *Getting to Yes*, by Roger Fisher and William Ury of the Harvard Negotiation Project (Fisher & Ury, 2011), will recognize the acronym BATNA, which stands for the "best alternative to a negotiated agreement." In other words, your selling squad should be able to define what you will do if you're unable to reach an agreement. Life will most certainly go on. As a salesperson, it's natural to see only your individual interests in a deal. Consider the broader interests of your organization in this deal; perhaps it is penetrating a new channel, a new geographic territory, winning a new account, increasing your share or wallet with a customer, or shutting out the competition from this account. There is always another pathway to each of these interests. Knowing those pathways, and sharing them with your team, allows your selling squad to feel confident and poised at those moments when others cave.

Negotiating is an advanced selling skill. Multiparty negotiations fall more in the territory of experienced lawyers than they do for salespeople. What's most important here as a selling squad leader is for you to appreciate the complexity. This awareness will cause you to tread carefully and coach your team to do the same. Breaking it down into pieces, gaining more information before responding, stressing value, and seeking one-on-one opportunities to focus on price enable you to handle tricky pricing questions in stride.

CHAPTER 16

NOTES TO SELF

1. Key points to remember about managing a price negotiation with a selling squad:

   a. _____

   b. _____

   c. _____

2. Opportunity for which you are currently building a selling squad:

   _____

   What actions will you take, and by when, to manage this discussion effectively?

   a. By planning for it during Organize? _____

   b. By simulating it during Practice? _____

   c. During Execute? _____

   d. By assessing it during Re-group? _____

3. To improve your long-term sales impact, you would like to:

   a. Stop: _____

   b. Start: _____

   c. Continue: _____

BOOSTING YOUR TEAM'S SELLING ENERGY

Each selling squad member brings to a sales call or pitch a certain level and kind of energy. I refer to this as "selling energy." Your selling energy on any given day may run the gamut from tortoise to hare.

Reflect on the last selling squad you put together. During Execute, how was your team's selling energy? What was each person's selling energy? And how did your team's individual and collective energy impact the outcome of the sales pitch or meeting?

Movie director Woody Allen has been quoted as saying that 80 percent of success in life is showing up. You've put great time and effort into coordinating your team's collective knowledge, planning, and practice. How you and your team "show up" to perform on game day is just as important.

Personal Selling Energy

Take this quick True/False quiz to help determine your personal selling energy:

1. I need coffee to get going in the morning.
2. I often zone in and out of client meetings.
3. I crave carbs and snacks to keep me going through the day.

4. I tend to feel sluggish mid-afternoon.
5. I get headaches and don't go anywhere without a bottle of aspirin or pain relievers.
6. I feel tired but wired at the end of the day and average fewer than eight hours of uninterrupted sleep.

How many trues did you score? Because you are a high-achieving sales professional, you may have missed that for this quiz, you were aiming for a low score. The fewer trues you counted, the better.

How do you think your last selling squad would have scored as a group?

Selling Energy in Sales Meetings

Presence, or your ability to be present and not absent, impacts your ability to conduct an effective meeting. Sales professionals tend to enjoy adrenaline and action and are generally not known for their heaping amounts of patience. And so it may follow that one or more members of that selling squad were large consumers of coffee or other caffeinated energy drinks, fast food, and energy snacks high in sugar or carbs. If this is true, some or all of the time, let's look at how this translates into the energy level you bring to a meeting.

Reflect on your recent client meetings. How often did your selling energy include some or all of the following feelings: tired, foggy, irritable, impatient, and anxious? Consider the ways in which these feelings may have impacted the meeting. Consider how they may have detracted from your efforts at building trust, credibility, and commitment.

Now, let's take a set of feelings opposite to those above—for example, energetic, focused, positive, patient, and steady. How would this kind of selling energy have changed the tone and set the stage for more effective sales meetings?

With greater awareness, you can connect your selling energy to what you eat, drink, or do before, during, or after an effective sales meeting. You may have the opportunity as a selling squad leader, depending on your selling squad's openness to the concept of "wellness," to model and influence more powerful selling energy in sales meetings. Holistic health coach and founder of Crave Nutrition Sandy Dalis helps clients, including professional salespeople, make a connection between what they consume and the direct effects on their sleep, mood, energy, and overall well-being. She suggests the following steps to boost selling energy:

- **Get a good night's sleep:** Do this not just the night before a big pitch but on a regular basis. How many hours of sleep do you typically get on a weeknight?

  The National Sleep Foundation reports that, "when we sleep well, we wake up feeling refreshed and alert for our daily activities. Sleep affects how we look, feel and perform on a daily basis, and can have a major impact on our overall quality of life." (National Sleep Foundation, 2015)

  We need "at least 8 hours a night of uninterrupted sleep to leave our bodies and minds rejuvenated for the next day. If sleep is cut short, the body doesn't have time to complete all of the phases needed for muscle repair, memory consolidation and release of hormones regulating growth and appetite. Then we wake up less prepared to concentrate, make decisions, or engage fully." (National Sleep Foundation, 2015)

  Contrary to some workaholic perceptions, the time that we spend sleeping is far from "unproductive." Sleep plays a direct role in how full, energetic, and successful your life can be. Get the sleep your body needs to be your best self and arrive focused and present. (Dalis, "Interview with Sandy Dalis," 2015)

- **Manage alcohol consumption:** It's not my goal here to judge or be "Danny Downer." Alcohol has become the glue that bonds many colleagues—especially for a selling squad the night before a pivotal customer meeting, since they rarely get to see one another. It's important to know that alcohol disturbs sleep patterns. This, in turn, can affect your focus, mood, and ability to execute the following day. There may be fewer stories to tell in the office, but you will be thankful you won the business by going light or passing altogether the night before an important sales meeting.

- **Hydrate:** Americans are chronically dehydrated. Many of us respond to this feeling by reaching for a cup of coffee or some other form of caffeine. This is ironic because dehydration can cause headaches, heartburn, anxiety, moodiness, and insomnia, which doesn't help with tip #1. Hydration experts, including Dr. Fereydoon Batamanghelidj, suggest setting a daily goal of drinking one-half your weight in water ounces. (For example, someone weighing 150 pounds should target drinking 75 ounces of water daily.) (Batamanghelidj, 2008)

- **Eat healthy:** If for a full day Practice meeting the morning session involves coffee and donuts, and your lunch includes fast food, consider this: eating nutritionally deficient food promotes illness and provides inadequate fuel to keep you going.

  Fast food is, well, fast. It is convenient in that it allows team members to eat quickly while preparing for or getting to the meeting. How you eat impacts how you perform. Sandy Dalis recommends avoiding "fake," heavy, fat-laden meals that make you feel sluggish. Rather, eat a healthy meal of "real food," packed with sustainable energy like healthy protein. Consuming your meal at least 45 minutes prior to a meeting avoids indigestion and hunger pangs. (Dalis, "Interview with Sandy Dalis," 2015)

  Another note about food. Foods with strong odors, like garlic, onions, or curry, can distract your customer or colleagues.

- **Breathe:** Take a nice big inhale—yes, right now, inhale deeply . . . and exhale completely. Do it again. How does that feel? When was the last time you did that? Sometimes we are so busy and stressed we actually forget to breathe. Dr. Andrew Weil explains that "Practicing regular, mindful breathing can be calming and energizing and can even help with stress-related health problems ranging from panic attacks to digestive disorders." (Weil, n.d.)

When you make the connection between how you live and how you feel, you will be on your way to harnessing the power of your selling energy. So, challenge yourself and encourage your team to pick and commit to one or more of the healthy practices above. Small steps lead to big changes, and the outcomes at stake here are significant.

CHAPTER 17

NOTES TO SELF

1. Key points to remember about managing your team's and your own selling energy:

   a. _____

   b. _____

   c. _____

2. Opportunity for which you are currently building a selling squad:

   _____

   What actions will you take, and by when, to manage your team's and your own selling energy:

   a. During Organize? _____

   b. During Practice? _____

   c. During Execute? _____

   d. During Re-group? _____

3. To improve your long-term sales impact, you would like to:

   a. Stop: _____

   b. Start: _____

   c. Continue: _____

CHAPTER 18 ———————————————

CREATING A MORE COLLABORATIVE CULTURE IN YOUR ORGANIZATION

In his book, *Team of Teams*, (Ret.) General Stanley McChrystal talks about how the military structure in Iraq had to adapt to a decentralized enemy in Al-Qaeda. This involved not only the creation of cross-functional units that could be deployed (teams). It meant that the command structure also needed to be cross-functional (team of teams). (McChrystal, 2015)

Selling organizations clearly are different from military organizations whose aim is to vanquish an enemy. The crossover point between General McChrystal's team of teams approach and selling squads is that conditions required a change in strategy (Part I of this book), and that groups that had previously eyed each other with suspicion were forced to find ways to work together effectively in smaller units to accomplish the broader mission (Part II of this book).

In this chapter of Part III, we begin to talk about what barriers to collaboration may exist in your organization. And how you can create change in order to drive better teamwork so that you can win more significant opportunities.

You may be aware of many barriers in your organization that prevent the kind of collaboration we have been discussing in this book. In a *New York Times* interview, Lars Dalgaard, general partner of the $4 billion venture capital firm Andreesen Horowitz, was asked about what he looks for in a company's culture. His response was, "If you can get organizational siloes to talk to each other, then you can have power in your organization." (Bryant, 2015) If you could find ways to remove these barriers, how much easier, more fun, and more effective would it be to build excellent selling squads?

If you're a senior leader or sales manager, we will talk in this chapter about some of the ways you can begin changing your organizational setting to facilitate the sort of teamwork that produces better selling squad performance. Doing that sets the stage for more effective cross-selling and enterprise-selling.

If you're a salesperson who leads or contributes to selling squads, we will cover actions you can take starting today that will begin changing the type of collaboration you experience.

Barriers to Cross-Organization Collaboration

To set the proper context for all of these ideas, it's important to first understand what you're up against by identifying the barriers commonly faced by leaders and salespeople.

Imagine this . . .

Your organization has successfully executed its business plan and grown dramatically, and it now encompasses more than 20 lines of business, solution areas, or disciplines. You hear about the importance of cross-selling and, in fact, it is one of the metrics against which you will be measured next year. You also feel the pressure to drive revenue to higher and higher levels as your company recovers from the financial crisis and must show returns on the investments it has made in building out new business lines —through talent and business acquisitions. People from other areas of the business are feeling the same pressure, as you are deluged by calls to gain access to several of your clients and people you know well. And those are the cordial ones.

Maybe the more aggressive salespeople from other parts of your company show little regard for connecting with you and learning about the client relationship you have built and instead, contact the company directly, which in your opinion, hurts your own credibility as well as the firm's. It may feel like anarchy at times. With the firm's larger clients, or key accounts, your organization may have put together account planning "teams." These groups are large, especially for the best client relationships; and the discussion is probably focused on completing a template for senior management and ensuring that all possible products or services that could be sold to them are included. When asked, you may have tried your best to coordinate introductions between your colleagues from other disciplines and the right people at the client company. In the process, you may also discover that your colleagues seem to have some widely different ideas about sales process and execution. As a result, these introductions tend not to go very well or far beyond that first meeting. You're not sure what to do.

That scenario reflects what often happens when an organization finds its own structure to be out of sync with its desired behaviors. In this case, as the account manager, you sincerely desire to do the right thing and have the capability and interest to lead an effective account team. Yet, you may find yourself surrounded by disjointed energy and activity.

In my research, coaching work, and experience, there are a number of common barriers to building effective teamwork among account teams reflecting different product or practice areas within the organization and across different functional roles. They all branch off the same issue: organizational structure. In fact, consultants Baker Tilly published a 2014 white paper in which the authors posit that "siloed structures are inherent in many organizations and are not conducive to effective collaboration and cross-selling." (Hanson, et al., 2014, p. 2)

Lines of business or practice areas may be a logical and efficient way to manage the enterprise. Before we discuss the various ways that you can drive collaboration, consider the ways in which silos impede teamwork among different departments:

■ **Wide spectrum of sales effectiveness:** Talent recruiting and development is left by many organizations to their various divisions. This enables leadership at the divisional level to decide the types of skills, behaviors, and experiences they seek in candidates. This structure also allows decisions to be made on what type of development, if any, is needed within that part of the organization. It is not hard to imagine that, across divisions, there exist different philosophies about selling and client-facing activities, among other things. One division believes in the star producer model and that the best thing management can do is get out of the way so this division can close deals. Another line of business believes that sales is process driven, and rallies around a sales process, best practices, and skills training. To the extent that divisional leaders disagree on the value of teamwork and collaboration, one can easily see how two people from different lines of business within the same organization can arrive at the same meeting with conflicting ideas about how it should be managed.

- **Different P&Ls:** One of the greatest levers a leader can pull is that of his or her budget. Allowing budgets to be created and managed by divisions gives each leadership team the ability to use resources as the team sees fit given the division's goals. So the budget is a reflection of the team's beliefs about driving revenue and managing costs. Training budgets, typically part of divisional budgets, also allow skill gaps that exist between divisions to grow over time.

- **Divergent access to technology, information, and tools:** Sitting in the present day, think about how networked you are personally and professionally, how much more quickly information flows to and from you compared to even 10 years ago. There has been tremendous adoption of customer relationship management (CRM) platforms and, with them, far greater ability for information sharing and analytics. Now what if, say, one line of business religiously uses a CRM and its people are well networked within their own division. Yet the information sharing does not go beyond this division to and from the company's other lines of business. Even with an enterprise-wide platform, information gained by one division may not be shared when different parts of the business pressure to compete rather than collaborate with one another. How would these types of scenarios impact selling squad collaboration before and teamwork during a customer meeting? In fact, Salesforce, in its "2015 State of Sales" research study, surveyed more than 2,300 global sales leaders across industries. Among their findings was that high-performing organizations are three times more likely than underperformers to view sales as an organization-wide, rather than an individual, responsibility. (Salesforce, 2015)

- **Competing goals:** Across different organizational siloes—whether they be by discipline or by functional role—objectives are set to advance their goals. Those objectives generally flow down the reporting lines and into performance goals, against which individuals are evaluated and compensated. What if the performance goals differ across divisions, as they likely will? What if one division, which has set enterprise-selling as a target, includes teamwork as a qualitative component in performance reviews, while another division sets goals that exclude any mention of team-based, cross-discipline, multiproduct, or cross-selling activity? Consider how that impacts a selling squad leader in recruiting group members and turning them into a team for an effective sales or client meeting.

  Matrix reporting lines can represent even greater confusion for individual team members. When the multiple masters they serve harbor different goals, they must reconcile them in choosing how to structure their activities.

- **Varied geographies, culture, and language:** Think about the many ways in which organizations deploy their sales, marketing, and support resources. Certain functions may be centralized, others distributed. Especially after the most recent economic crisis in 2007–2008, many organizations worked to protect their profit margins by redefining roles and avoiding—or at least minimizing—duplication of resources. This experience also refocused many companies on driving revenue from more sources. This caused many companies to expand distribution into new channels and new geographic markets. For an intact team all located in the same office, this is tough enough to pull off. When resources are distributed, think about how much harder it has become to assemble a team—keeping up with all the capabilities you need, finding people whom you can partner with, and then pulling them together onto a selling squad. You must now be able to factor in and navigate around a higher cost of sales, greater travel time, and higher communication barriers.

- **Different rewards:** Across the enterprise, there may be wildly different ideas about how rewards should be structured. Rewards could be financial and be reflected in the form of a compensation program design, or even nonfinancial, including what behaviors are acknowledged. Compensation consultants ZS Associates reflected on their work in developing more than 700 sales force compensation plans and found that "when poorly designed or implemented, these (incentive compensation) models can result in dramatically inflated cost of sales, destructive conflict between team members, weakened accountability for results and high levels of customer confusion." (Moorman & Albrecht, 2008, p. 33) They explain that a poorly designed comp program cannot counter "tension regarding what is the right customer solution, who has decision authority and who should be involved in a given opportunity." but instead leads to suboptimal outcomes all around. (Moorman & Albrecht, 2008, p. 34) Yet, many leaders over-rely on their comp program and hope that their teams will somehow find their way to collaboration and team selling success. Harvard professor Heidi Gardner, whose research focuses on professional services firms, feels that all of the following can discourage collaboration: commissions, producer recognition groups like "president's club," third-party star-ranking lists, and even what sales wins get the spotlight in firm-wide meetings and communications discourage collaboration. (Gardner, *HBR*, 2015, p. 78)

- **Inconsistent leadership messages:** Oftentimes, senior leaders want to forge change in how their organization collaborates to capture the benefits of team selling—including larger, cross-discipline mandates that carry a lower acquisition cost and better senior-level access. Yet, what gets communicated is at odds with the goal. John Kotter, Harvard Business School professor and author of *Leading Change*, has found that the majority of change efforts fail, largely due to inconsistent messaging and lack of leadership support. (Kotter, 2014)

So how do you get beyond these obstacles in trying to win more consistently when selling squads are the required path to get you there?

Organizational Climate

The research on high-performing teams is unequivocal: the organizational setting in which teams perform is a major factor in going from group to team. It is what Susan Wheelan calls "organizational support" (Wheelan, 2010, p. 2), what Richard Hackman refers to as the "enabling structure" (Hackman, 2002, p. 93), and what LaFasto and Larson label the "the organizational environment." (LaFasto & Larson, 2001, p. 157) Boston Consulting Group, in its white paper "The Three Golden Rules of Cross-Selling," state their position that "the fundamental driver of cross-selling is getting the *organization* right." (Cainey, et al., 2002, p. 1)

As I share some ideas for you to consider in your own organization, I will group them into those that apply to leaders in considering top-down adjustments; and those that can be leveraged by selling squad members—team leaders, subject matter experts, and even extended group members—to modify their own actions from the bottom up within the organization.

For Senior and Sales Managers

Let's start organizationally from the top down. Getting the organization right, to use Boston Consulting Group's phrase, involves looking at three components—communication, coaching, and compensation—within your own organization to see if they are contributing to or

FIGURE 18.1 Three C's of Building Organizational Collaboration

COMMUNICATION	COACHING	COMPENSATION

detracting from your desire to facilitate better teamwork across your own organization—for the purpose of producing more effective cross-selling and, even further, true enterprise-wide or cross-discipline solutions for clients across your organization's channels and geographical footprint. (See Figure 18.1.)

Communication

There are two components of management communication that I'd like to address here—from senior managers down into their groups, and for managers across the organization's divisions, whether they be separated by product, business line, and/or geography.

Referring back to Kotter's work on change leadership, if as a leader you strive for your organization to be among the minority that successfully creates change, what message you deliver, and how and when you communicate it, are all significant components. (Kotter, 2014) Communicating generic messages that vary by leader and seem to come and go with the wind conveys one thing quite clearly: whatever you are attempting to communicate is being received as not relevant and not important and will disappear as quickly as it arrived.

Asking managers and their people to change current behavior is big. People engage in their activities because they believe them to be—rightly or wrongly—linked to producing results and success. Operating in a way that differs from their current path is risky: it may not work, they may be embarrassed in front of colleagues, and they may fear failure, which could cost them compensation and even their job. One of the biggest mistakes I see leaders make in forging any change initiative—including to promote more teamwork—is to use what I like to call the Bruce Willis method of management communication: toss it like a grenade over the shoulder and walk away. Communicating the need for behavior change in individuals must be clear and compelling; connected to the organization's goals, challenges, and initiatives; consistent within the team and across the organization; and specific to individuals. And repeating messages allows full absorption by the recipient.

Let's unpack that. Messaging effectively requires empathy. Ernest Wilson III, dean of University of Southern California's Annenberg School for Communication and Journalism, states that empathy, compared to all the other leadership attributes most commonly cited in his research among business executives, was most important. (Wilson, 2015) Let's play this out from the top down. This means that as the CEO, you are able to convey to your senior leadership team an understanding for their concerns about changing current practices; that your senior leaders are able to do the same within their own management teams; and that your first-line managers are able to empathize and message as well.

For a leader to be clear and compelling in his or her messaging sounds about as disagreeable as motherhood and apple pie could. What does it really mean? The message that begins with the CEO and flows down and across the organization is simple and important. This requires preparation, practice, and feedback to ensure that what gets received aligns with your intent. This transmits through your organization that regardless of what was understood in the past, it is no longer acceptable to act as a solo performer and sends the message that there is a new expectation of teamwork both within and across business lines.

Why devote space in your messaging to the organization's goals, challenges, and initiatives? Two reasons: (1) this is another opportunity to remind people that there are goals, challenges, and initiatives; and (2) you set the context within which team-based selling is important. For example:

- **Goal:** "As you know, we are aiming to grow the organization organically by 10 percent over the next two years."
- **Challenge:** "This is not going to be a cakewalk. Competition has grown in every direction, and we have several product gaps and deficiencies."

- **Initiative:** "This is why the leadership team has put together an initiative to promote and monitor cross-product collaboration across the organization."

The message must also be specific to the audience with whom you are communicating. This group might be large, as in the case of a companywide or national sales meeting; it might be a small group, as in the case of a specific team; or it might even be one person, as part of a scheduled one-on-one meeting. Regardless of the audience's size, what is your ask? You may want people to work together differently, perhaps within their own selling squads, and maybe with others across the broader organization. Consider what success would look like for you. Perhaps it is people committing time, especially over the next 120 days, to prepare together longer and more intentionally. Maybe you would like to see people broadening their contacts by the end of this year across the company that will strengthen their solution set and increase the number of potential partners that can help craft, explain, and deliver solutions that cross organizational lines.

Effective messaging is also consistent. This means a few things. First, a similar version of the message that a manager hears in one part of the company squares with what a friend, who leads a team in another division, also hears. Second, it means that the message is repeated. It's been said that for messages to be fully understood they need to be repeated five to seven times. Even if the team you lead is a group of brilliant PhDs in molecular biology, repeated messaging allows them to gain increasing focus as they filter out other thoughts, and be certain that this is one of those messages that is here to stay. Third, connected with your specific ask, check in consistently to seek among your leaders, managers, and individual performers evidence and examples of consistent, collaborative, and cross-organizational behavior change. What examples are they able to cite of selling teams preparing together differently? What evidence can they provide of meetings they have held with people outside their past internal network, and what commitments to collaborate were made?

The final component of communication is the action you take as a leader to facilitate collaboration on your team, with channel partners, and across the organization. These might include:

- **A CRM tool deployed across the organization:** Incomplete deployment limits communication and collaboration. If in your own little part of the world, you consistently communicate your expectation that people leverage the CRM tool that you've deployed, it will get used. With that as a starting point, there are a number of functionality tools within most CRMs that allow selling squads to effect knowledge leveling across their core or extended team colleagues, and to help bring others into the fold to advance existing opportunities, retain existing client mandates, and find and plan around new ones.

- **Bilateral networking events:** Forging a relationship with another business line that you have done very little work with in the past offers benefits on two levels. On one level, it is an opportunity for you as a leader to model your request for new and better collaboration. It also provides a platform where your people can better understand another capability and become better acquainted with the people you would be partnering with. On the first point, a lunch-and-learn format is widely used to broadcast product or service type of information. In my experience, these events can succeed or fail based on the effectiveness of one sales rep who is delivering his or her standard internal cross-sell pitch. Consider partnering him or her with one or more people from your own team to properly prepare for the opportunity and to be sure comments are customized, including the benefits, to your team and the market you cover. You could also consider organizing a networking event, such as a happy hour that allows the individuals on your team to connect with one or more individuals on another team. Successful teams are built on a foundation of credibility and trust. Providing the platform for people to connect personally and professionally allows them to begin developing credibility and trust in one another. This is essential if they are going to consider entrusting each other with something as precious as an introduction to a client relationship they have built, in some cases, over many years.

- **Recognition:** Be intentional with the success stories you broadcast to your teams in group meetings, in calls, or via other forms of communications. If you are messaging more teamwork but always seem to highlight successes that attach to one person, you can see how that can sabotage your own efforts for behavior change. Find small wins to start, and look for larger ones as they happen. Recognize these wins in team settings, being sure to discuss in advance with the people responsible for that win so that it is messaged in a way that works well for you both. And in one-on-one settings, be sure to acknowledge even unsuccessful attempts at new behaviors. Done properly, this rewards progress toward a desired behavior and, unlike changes to a compensation plan, is done easily and at no cost.

How can a management team communicate a message consistently if it doesn't agree as a leadership team in the substance of the message? As it relates to team selling, this could reflect different views on the importance of preparation, practice, post-mortems, cross-selling, enterprise-wide or cross-discipline solutions, training, one CRM, and so on. This is the point at which a management team shows whether it operates as a high-performing team or simply a group of individual performers. Among the many lessons in this book, consider how high-performing teams rally behind a unified performance goal and seek, not consensus, but rather how to work through conflict and to forge agreement, giving decision rights to those on the team who are best positioned to make that call. It is important to set time for the team to discuss and debate the topic, so it can get to a place of appreciation on the importance of better teamwork. This is not a "let's all sit in a circle, join hands, and sing 'Kumbaya' activity" or a "fall backward and see if others will catch you exercise." Rather, this is an important path to accomplish the management or leadership team's mission. Expect conflict. Managers get to a position of authority based on the strong views they hold. Resolve these conflicts in private and seek unified commitment on the message as an outcome.

Coaching

After you communicated your message, you checked in for evidence and examples of take-up on your ask. Invariably there will be gaps between your expectations—what you thought you communicated—and the behaviors and activity you see. These gaps form the input for coaching, the second of the three C's of setting an appropriate organizational climate. How do you do it effectively?

You know the story . . . as a mild-mannered sales manager, you have a one-on-one meeting with an ordinary sales citizen to check in on how this citizen has changed his or her process for creating and leading selling squads. A problem arises and—WHAM!—you make a beeline to the phone booth (yes, they still exist) and out comes super sales manager, complete with red cape. (Did you think superhuman abilities were limited to the super sellers we discussed in Chapter 1?) Faster than a speeding sales cycle, more powerful than a strong pipeline, and able to leap tall revenue goals in a single bound. In your rush to rescue Metropolis and solve the salesperson's dilemma, however, you may not realize that this method of coaching for sales teams is not really coaching at all; it is kryptonite to your team's performance.

Before we talk about how to properly provide sales coaching to a team leader or team, it's important to be aware of several dynamics at play:

- Salespeople and selling teams come to you with a wide range of skills and talents. They know at least one thing far better than you do: themselves.
- As a sales manager, you probably came to the position based on your success as a salesperson. You likely take pride in how you used to help clients. Now that you're in a management role, you genuinely want to help your team by sharing with them your experience and insights.
- How you "help" salespeople may create unintended consequences:
  - Being the superhero problem solver is not scalable, and leads to manager burnout.

- Solving the immediate problem, while expedient, makes your team dependent (rather than independent), reduces their sense of ownership, stunts their results and professional growth, and slows down the sales process.

Asking—rather than telling—takes patience and restraint, not natural strengths for most sales leaders. Effective sales managers realize that coaching for sales teams requires processes and skills that may be a departure from those you used in a selling role.

In my work with sales leaders, there is universal agreement that coaching is important and should be done more often. Many, however, don't fully appreciate how different the qualities needed to coach effectively are from simply leading. Who are the leaders you most admire? Who were your favorite coaches? Think for a moment about the qualities those leaders possessed, versus those of the mentors or coaches you have had in your life. Which of the following did you include? (See Figure 18.2.)

FIGURE 18.2 Leader vs. Coach Qualities

LEADERSHIP QUALITIES	COACHING/MENTOR QUALITIES
Charismatic	Empathetic
Strong	Understanding
Resolute	Supportive
Decisive	Believing
Impatient	Patient
Ambitious	Compassionate

Quite a gap, huh?

Coaching, in my view, falls under the heading of servant leadership. Since the 1970s, the topic of servant leadership has largely been ascribed to management thinker Robert Greenleaf. (Greenleaf, 1977) The concept has ancient roots and involves a leader's belief in his or her mission and people, over oneself and one's own ambitions. In the case of sales leadership, it involves turning the organization chart upside-down, so that the client supersedes all—the sales organization seeks to serve the client, and the leader serves the client indirectly through his or her work supporting the sales team.

SERVANT LEADERSHIP AND COACHING

An effective leader who is also an effective coach is aware of those moments when you are performing one role versus the other. (See Figure 8.3.) The levers you learn to pull in order to downshift into coaching mode are patience and restraint, regardless of whether your direct reports are salespeople who lead selling squads, or sales managers who manage a team of salespeople who at times create selling squads. You may find this difficult at first, but it takes a good process and practice to do effectively—remember, your sense of urgency and action orientation are prized as a leader. Patience and restraint may not be qualities that your manager was seeking when he or she first

FIGURE 18.3 Traditional vs. Servant Leadership

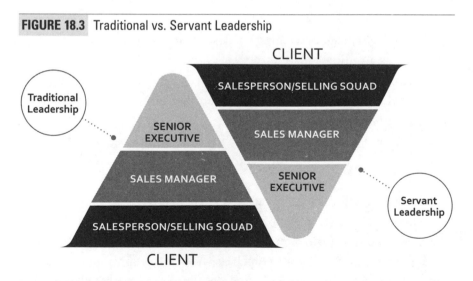

Where traditional leadership models organize around the leader, a servant leadership model puts your client and customer-facing staff as the focus; with management supporting that interaction.

hired you as a sales leader; in fact, he or she may have been looking for the opposite. Possessing a willingness to jump in quickly and knowing when to do so can be invaluable when, for example, you're setting strategy for a struggling business unit and when providing leadership to a team going through industry or organizational change. When coaching sales teams, however, you need to be able to find and draw on both of these qualities: patience, to provide space for the salesperson or selling squad to self-discover the issues, causes, and solutions; and restraint, to hold yourself back from putting on your super sales manager cape and solving the problem and therefore missing the opportunity to build the salesperson's independence and investment in change.

DEVELOPMENTAL SALES COACHING

How do you share developmental coaching feedback? Recall that we talked in Chapter 8 about the importance of giving and receiving balanced, specific, and honest feedback and in Chapter 9 about how to share peer-to-peer feedback in a selling squad's Practice session.

Developmental coaching is typically done between a manager and a direct report. For example, this could include these scenarios:

- A sales manager coaching a salesperson on how to grow stronger as a selling squad leader
- A manager of a product area coaching a subject matter expert (SME) on how to elevate his or her contributions to a selling squad meetings
- A senior executive coaching a line of business leader on how to create more collaboration across business lines

Developmental coaching tends to be longer term in nature than the type of peer-to-peer feedback that is limited to one's contributions to a specific pitch, for example. This type of coaching focuses on one developmental area at a time—such as, how to conduct more effective Organize meetings—to foster incremental and sustainable change that may take several coaching sessions. And developmental coaching is best managed between trusted parties.

Good coaches are also willing to receive feedback on their coaching. Be willing to empower your direct reports with the same process and guidelines. Who knows? The master may become the student and vice versa.

Without a process, you may find that as a manager you stumble your way through coaching conversations. Servant leaders find their way to a process that works but, speaking from my own journey as a manager, trial and error can be painful for all involved and take time that you don't have. You may be the kind of leader who is quick to ditch coaching until you are shown a process that works, get the space and support to practice it, and are asked regularly by your own manager for evidence and examples of your coaching experiences and results (as discussed above in the first of the three C's: communication). Moving to a more team-based selling process is an example of behavior change that may be significant for many in your organization. As mentioned, behavior change can feel scary and risky, especially when it affects compensation, promotion, and even employment decisions. Engaged coaching is the medium to help people feel confident enough to bridge that gap.

THE HOW, WHY, AND WHAT OF DEVELOPMENTAL COACHING

The words *how*, *why*, and *what*—in that order—are far more powerful tools in coaching sales teams than are speed, power, and leaping ability. (See Figure 18.4.)

Let's look at how each of these three words prompts an important question in an effective sales coaching dialogue with one of your managers, selling squad leaders, or contributors:

- **How:** How did your selling squad perform during the sales call? How are your selling squad leaders progressing in their ability to create winning selling squads? How do you see the trends changing in your division's win rates on the larger, more complex deals that require multiple selling partners? The *how* question leads, or forces in some cases, self-reflection by the manager, salesperson, or contributor. For you as a coach, it provides a view into your colleague's level of awareness.

FIGURE 18.4 Feedback Dialogue

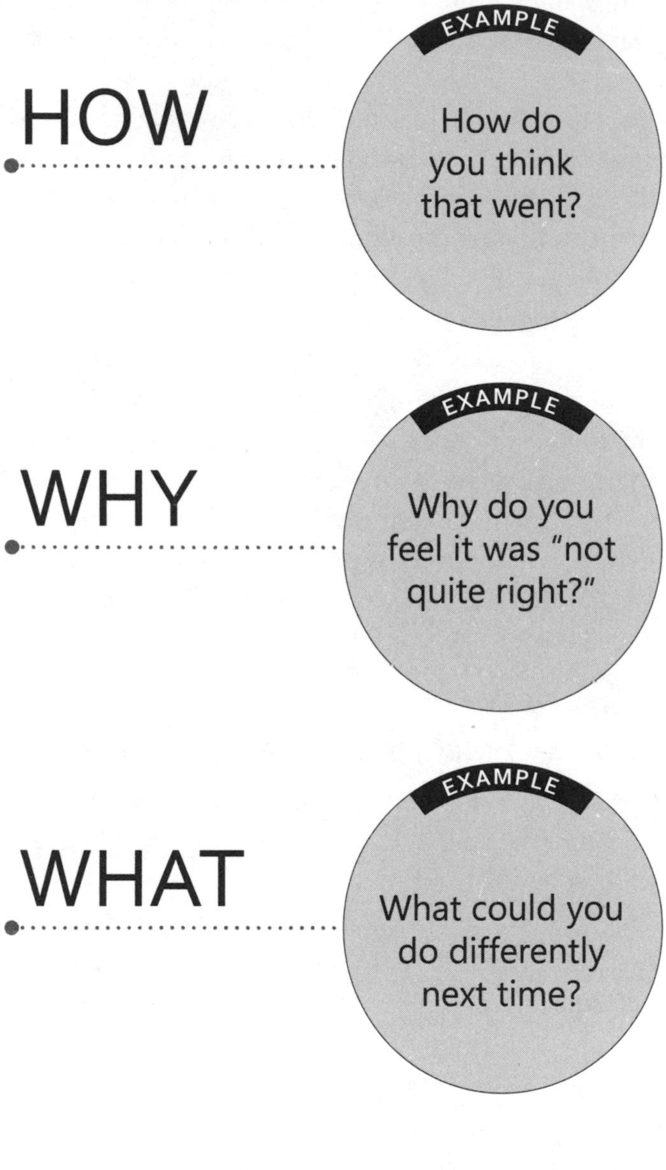

HOW

EXAMPLE

How do you think that went?

WHY

EXAMPLE

Why do you feel it was "not quite right?"

WHAT

EXAMPLE

What could you do differently next time?

- **Why:** Why do you feel progress has been slow? Why was the team able to create that result? Why are we not seeing even stronger win rates? The *why* question allows you to guide the manager, salesperson, or contributor to identify the trigger that is causing the current state. As with your *how* question, asking a *why* question —rather than telling—provokes self-discovery and makes your colleague accountable for discovery.
- **What:** What are some ideas you could try to generate progress? What could you do to replicate this team's success? What actions could you take to escalate your group's win rate? The *what* question puts the manager, salesperson, or team in the driver's seat with regard to their own development. And working with the ideas they generate increases ownership and commitment to follow-through. You're able to monitor and watch—as servant leaders do—how the plan plays out, and are able to move on to other things.

Your *how, why,* and *what* questions initiate and guide dialogue. As a coach, your next-level managers, salespeople, or contributors will expect you to have a view as well, so you should come prepared with that. The important point here is that each question kicks off that part of the conversation. It allows the salesperson or team the space for self-discovery of the issues, drivers, and potential solutions—prior to your sharing your views on the how, why, and what of the situation.

BEST PRACTICES IN DEVELOPMENTAL SALES COACHING

Even the most super of super sales managers among us have been able to find within themselves patience and restraint, and to use the above questions, employing the following eight simple tips:

1. Set a clear objective for each sales coaching session, focusing on outcomes that will gain the change you need to accomplish your goals.
2. Prepare for sales coaching sessions, especially those *how, why.* and *what* questions that will guide the person you're coaching through a self-discovery process.

3. Provide a safe and supportive environment, encouraging honesty and reflection without judging, criticizing, or looking for "right" answers.
4. Listen more, talk less. One of the senior executives I coach writes two simple words on his notepad as a sales coaching reminder: "Shut up!"
5. Be more curious about each of your direct reports, and have the courage to ask "Why?" in response to their comments. Be willing to ask two to three questions before providing your views. You know from your own experience: people learn best from themselves.
6. Acknowledge that moving even an accomplished person out of a comfortable performance pattern will be, by definition, uncomfortable. Expect him or her to struggle, using silence when needed and providing support when appropriate.
7. See how developmental coaching benefits your team; including greater empowerment, independence, excitement, and vision to get to a higher performance level.
8. Realize what you gain by coaching your team; including increased skill level and performance from your team as well as more time for you to focus on higher value activities.

Coaching sales managers, selling squad leaders, and contributors is one of your key performance drivers as a manager. Leveraging it requires a process and some qualities you may not have needed to succeed in the past. So the next time you hear the cry for help from somewhere in Metropolis, hold off putting on the red cape and remind yourself that the ordinary sales citizen may just be smart enough to save himself or herself. In the process this will free up your time to tackle more important issues facing the great city.

WHO SHOULD BE COACHED?

Who in your organization needs coaching? Once you become accustomed to downshifting to coaching, and know how to do it, it's like having a true superpower that you want to use wherever possible because you know that—other than hire-fire decisions —it drives the most significant impact in results. On one level, the question of who to coach is easy. Of your direct reports, you coach those who want to be coached. As it relates to selling squads, team leaders tend to need it the most. Because with every new opportunity and pivotal meeting, there may be a different team that needs to be created and organized. But who should coach members of the selling squad that, because of their role or product area, fall outside the scope of your management? The most effective selling organizations with which I work create vibrant feedback cultures, where people are used to skillfully exchanging feedback with one another—whether their selling partner resides above, below, or to the side of them on an organization chart. People who participate on sales calls, leader or contributor, should be coached regularly to refine and improve their impact in team sales meetings.

DEAL COACHING VS. DEVELOPMENTAL COACHING

Another form of coaching is deal coaching. Someone outside the core team is recruited as a coach to guide the team on a winning path. An organization that promotes collaboration encourages selling squads to use a coach to provide a feedback loop, allowing the team to course correct as its work proceeds. A selling squad's coach can be internal or external, as discussed in Chapter 7.

WHEN SHOULD YOU COACH A SELLING SQUAD?

In this book, you have learned the process for building a winning selling squad—Create, Organize, Practice, Execute, Re-group. If you are a selling squad's designated coach, your role is to coach to gaps in the team's use of that process. There is an important role for you to play before and after that important client meeting. Consider participating in the team's Organize, Practice, and Re-group meetings. The coach should be serving the core team as it prepares as a unit. This can include providing feedback on their work on knowledge leveling; the state of their planning for materials and logistics; and for each team member given his or her performance during team Practice sessions.

According to Hackman, there are three types of coaching "interventions" that can impact team effectiveness: the energy team members are contributing to the collective effort, the strategy they are using to carry out their work, and the knowledge and skill they bring to the party. (Hackman, 2002, p. 167) In terms of how as a leader you coach selling squads, it's valuable to keep in mind two other concepts. First, you may recall Heidi Gardner's research with professional services firms from earlier in this book, and her findings that it's important to draw out and give weight to client knowledge, even when that knowledge is held by members of the selling squad who may hold junior roles in your firm relative to others on that team. (Gardner, 2012) Second, you may recall from earlier in the book my references to the work of MIT's Sandy Pentland in the arena of social physics. (Pentland, 2012) That notion of equal talk time can help you as a selling squad coach ensure that the team's decisions are based on all, not just the loudest, voices at the table. A coach can help guard against dominating influences in the group and solve for the free rider problem to ensure that the best ideas get surfaced by the people who are in the best position to know. This also helps make sure that the team is receiving equal contributions among its members and still factoring in external information.

Psychologist Ivan Steiner talks about "synergistic process gains and losses," where the collective produces up to or below its potential. (Steiner, 1972) Hackman posits that coaches should seek to coach around these process gains and losses, and that there are three times when teams seem to be most receptive to coaching interventions: at the start, in the middle of the team's collective work, and at the end of their work. (Hackman, 2002, p. 179) This confirms our earlier discussions on the importance of a selling squad's feedback loop, and clarifies the pivotal role an effective coach can play.

SELLING SQUAD COACHING INTERVENTIONS

Let's take another look at what a coach can do at each stage:

- During an Organize meeting or call, a coach can—directly with a selling squad or by supporting its leader—ensure the team is

aimed properly at the start, and help the team refine preliminary ideas and scan for new information that may have become
available since the selling squad's work together began.

■ During a Practice session—ideally scheduled far enough in
advance of a pitch or meeting—the coach can facilitate the
incorporation of feedback and new information in the selling
squad's final work.

■ During a Re-group meeting, the coach might enable the
team—before it disbands—to learn from their work together so
that the selling squad and its members grow more effective in
future outings.

Being an effective selling squad coach requires trust and credibility
with team members. We talked earlier about the importance, qualities,
and process for delivering peer-to-peer feedback effectively. That same
concept of delivering balanced, specific, and honest feedback while
leveraging the how, why, and what questions mentioned earlier, will
enable you as a selling squad's coach to effect a coaching intervention
for the team, its leader, or team members in a way that allows them to
maximize their impact on a high-stakes meeting and to grow professionally. When handled poorly, not only can a coaching intervention
throw a team off-course, it can also destroy trust and damage relationships. This is especially important to note if you as a manager seek to
coach people in your reporting structure.

WHERE SHOULD COACHING OCCUR?

Choosing an appropriate location for coaching is worth touching upon.
Intact teams whose members trust one another enough to allow feedback to be given and received collectively are rare. Short of that, team
feedback should not be given to the team as a collective. Individual
feedback on member contributions is best given one-on-one, in a private setting to ensure attention and receptivity. Team feedback should
also be delivered in a setting that minimizes onlookers and keeps everyone open and focused. When time is short, selling squads have a habit
of giving feedback as a collective. It is important to note that while this

process is expedient and usually feels good to the team leader, it is not the most effective way to produce behavior change among team members. Those who are struggling, and who may be outside their comfort zone already, may feel overwhelmed and this may further increase their sense of pressure. The result may be an even weaker performance during the client meeting than what would have been possible had they been coached in a safe setting.

WHO SHOULD COACH?

If your organizational climate facilitates strong collaboration, you and your fellow leaders and managers ought to be able to discuss and decide amongst yourselves, resolve any conflicts, and reach agreement on who coaches which selling squads, modeling the behaviors you seek on your own individual teams.

Hackman's view is "what is critical is that competent coaching is available to a team, regardless of who provides it or what formal position those providers hold." (Hackman, 2002, p. 194)

Selling squads have options in choosing a coach for their team. The team might have access to an internal coach who is a manager, designated sales coach, or salesperson outside the core and extended teams, or an external sales coach.

Internal or external, "competent" coaching means credibility. If you seek to coach a selling squad effectively, you should bring to your work with a selling squad the following six qualities:

1. You should have or be able to establish a trusting and trusted relationship with each member of the team.
2. You should be able to coach skillfully, bringing the qualities mentioned earlier including being supportive, patient, and discreet.
3. You should be experienced—to understand the domain in which the selling squad operates and to appreciate what an effective team sales meeting looks like.
4. You should be skillful and use an effective coaching process, akin to the one described above, that allows the team members to, first, learn from themselves and each other and, then, from

you as an engaged and insightful observer. Facilitating an internal feedback loop—with a team or one-on-one—enables the selling squad and its members to better meet their performance goal while growing professionally in the process.

5. You must be available. A great coach who is credible but too busy to engage as and when needed by the team in the lead-up to a critical sales meeting offers little value.

6. You must be objective. Because you reside outside the core and extended teams, you are able to deliver feedback that is unbiased and avoids a group's tendencies to fall in love with its own ideas.

Compensation

The final of the three C's is compensation. Even if you are not a compensation expert, you will probably recognize the truth behind the following two statements:

1. Not changing your compensation plan is unlikely to fully change behaviors.
2. Changing your compensation plan on its own is unlikely to fully change behaviors.

As it relates to compensation, an old manager of mine was fond of the saying, "You don't play games with people's comp." What's true about this statement is that money is a very personal topic. And changing how it's delivered can impact a person's current obligations and future plans. For many it also sends a message, intended or not, about their worth to you and your organization.

Those are not reasons to leave a compensation program in place that has fallen out of step with the realities of your business plan today and going forward. Choosing to not adjust the plan but expecting different behaviors is, well, wishful thinking. According to ZS Associates, "sales force incentives play a big role in reinforcing what's important." (Moorman & Albrecht, 2008, p. 33) It's hard to ignore the power of a leadership team that, as described above, is unified, relevant, specific, and engaged in its messaging about why behavior change is needed and what is expected; and supporting it with coaching. It's easy to see how a compensation plan that continues to reward individual performance focused on one's own silo might send an even more important message that people should carry on with their current behaviors.

On the other hand, changing a compensation plan alone to reward better teamwork in sales and customer meetings is equally unlikely to change behaviors. Picture this: a sales manager has violated the "don't play games with people's comp" rule and, through the changes, has sent some type of message about more collaboration, cross-selling, and team-based selling. Yet individual performers have succeeded based on the old rules, and they're all of a sudden being asked to change. They are not being told why change is needed, what they personally need to change in order to be effective, or how to accomplish it. In addition, the manager and his fellow leaders are changing none of their own behaviors in working together. The sales manager is neither addressing the risks his people feel about changing nor helping them, through engaged coaching, as they try to adapt to this new compensation plan.

You can see how these mismatches are likely to create all sorts of random results, including people gaming the system without any changes to their go-to-market behaviors, groups of people mangling the process of trying to work together, and solid individual performers deciding to jump ship after concluding that they are no longer wanted in this system.

Consultants Michael Moorman and Chad Albrecht from ZS Associates suggest the following best practices on sales incentive plans to facilitate better team selling across the organization:

- **Sales force structure:** This involves defining or redefining roles so that people can better understand what actions fall at their feet versus those of their colleagues. This might include appointing someone as a key account manager who helps the team organize its activities, including cross-selling and looking for broader opportunities that cross the different product areas in which individual team members are focused.
- **Sales process:** Helping people see the stages of a sale, and even the parts of a client-focused meeting or call, is foundational to

facilitating better collaboration. For some in your organization, this type of investment may seem like it's not needed since this is how they sell today. For others, it's urgent as the gaps have grown large between their product-pushing style and the way customers buy today and how other parts of your organization go to market. Despite the groaning, everyone will appreciate a unified process they can collaborate around for more effective sales meetings that produce more, different, and better opportunities.

- **Sales force deployment:** How well organized are resources in the field to allow for collaboration versus competition? Thought should be given to how people will cover a territory—whether that's defined by geography, channels, and/or accounts. Free-for-alls can be interesting to watch if you're not part of them. Define the ground rules for how teams will operate within that territory. Examples of this include key account team and "mirroring," which means representatives from different lines of business jointly own a territory.

- **Incentives:** ZS Associates shares the following best practices in aligning the compensation program with the above best practices to produce better collaboration in finding, developing, and managing accounts and opportunities:

  1. Make the plan simple to understand.
  2. Keep the group of metrics small (three priorities or fewer).
  3. Make the measures felt at the individual level. Setting a metric too broadly, say at the regional level, can be easy to administer but may feel too distant for any person within that region to impact. Structure incentives to pay out to the team's members when they achieve a performance goal set for a dedicated or "mirrored" account team. For organizations that are unable to structure teams in dedicated or mirrored territories, getting incentives right is trickier. Balancing levels of contribution to, and payment for, that success is tough to administer and can cause disagreements about who contributed how much to which sale.

4. Be sure that incentives line up with (1) overall compensation packages that remain competitive for specific markets and roles and (2) line of business goals so that associated members continue to stay focused on that line of business rather than promoting other product areas that may produce better incentives.

5. Align sales incentives with those of senior management to avoid conflicts between leadership and salesforce behaviors. (Moorman & Albrecht, 2002)

Communication, coaching, and compensation. These three C's allow you as a leader to set the organizational climate within which effective selling teamwork happens within your span of control.

Tips for Selling Squad Leaders and Members

The organizational setting in which groups are formed—for selling and other work tasks—play a big role in creating the conditions that allow your selling squads to come together as high-performing teams. The company you represent exists in its current state; change, as described here, requires leadership teamwork, time, shared commitment, and energy. As a passionate client advocate, you realize that there must be actions you can take today with your colleagues that will produce better outcomes in this new selling environment, and within your organization to influence change that will lead to better conditions for teamwork across disciplines.

Let's look first at things you can own today that will produce better outcomes in your selling squad meetings.

Build Your Network

Many professional services firms, for example, have grown in their appreciation for how important internal relationships are in producing better client outcomes. They encourage and provide forums for networking. The more consultants within a firm know one another, the more effective they can be in building engagement teams well suited for client needs and identifying opportunities to serve clients outside their own discipline. Even in such firms, many consultants focus only on the work, rather than both the work and the relationships that will allow them to find and deliver that work. You don't have to work for a consulting firm to begin adopting this best practice.

What if you work for an organization that neither encourages nor facilitates internal networking? Uh, you're a sales or client-facing professional, you make your living figuring whom you need to connect with at client organizations and then getting after it. Building your internal network takes the same sort of discipline. As with prospecting, this is not networking for networking sake; it has intention. How well do you know your organization's capabilities? Who are those people connected to far-flung capabilities that would help you to better understand what customer demand that capability is tapping into? Knowing those people will allow you to bring a broader scope to client meetings. And, when appropriate, these same people may be instrumental in developing solutions to client needs that cross your organization's product siloes. They can also become a part of a selling squad that prepares and practices with you as a cohesive team in making a compelling and winning case to a client. None of these things can happen without a broad network within your organization.

Invest in Your Internal Relationships

We touched on this subject in Chapter 5 when we discussed the importance of developing mutual trust and credibility as a foundation for strong selling partner relationships. Consider the time, thought, and energy you invest in cultivating external relationships. You initiate contact, you stay in touch, you prepare, you seek to understand them better professionally and personally, you help them accomplish their goals so that you can reach yours, you follow up diligently. How does that compare with the way in which you manage your internal relationships?

Most sales professionals, when asked, admit there is a large gap between the two. And it is easy to see why. On its surface, you as a client-facing professional are deployed and compensated to go out and gain distribution for the products and services that your company offers. Your sales manager encourages you to build external relationships since, as many sales managers are fond of saying: "You don't meet your next million-dollar prospect in your office or living room." Your manager may even try to promote more calling activity by including in your goals specific metrics for prospect, customer, and center of influence (referral source) meetings or calls. So it can feel as if time spent with internal colleagues is unproductive and takes you away from meeting your sales goals.

One successful salesperson I coached told me a story about a company she worked for. Leadership prohibited her from being in the office between 10 a.m. and 4 p.m. and installed a GPS tracking device on her car so they could see her whereabouts whenever they desired. When she visited another office belonging to that company or its affiliates, she was instructed to "stop wasting her time." It's hard, even for a thick-skinned salesperson, to not get frustrated by contrasting messages of sell more and sell bigger with sell solo.

At one extreme, consider first that if you are out of the office all day, every day, you will likely exceed your activity metrics for sales calls. Where you may falter, however, is cross-selling other parts of the company and finding larger enterprise sales.

At the other extreme, let's say you're a salesperson who has a great internal network, and knows everyone in the company. You are considered a great team player and are given high marks for referrals you make to other parts of the company. However, perhaps your pipeline is relatively empty, your win rate is low, and your calling activity is far below the activity metrics set for your position.

How do you find the optimal point between those two extremes and enable yourself to keep your internal relationships and knowledge current, while executing a sales calling plan that connects this network into the best external opportunities? There is certainly a lot of room between these extremes. Taking into account how the market has changed, and even how your own organization has evolved over time, is it possible to update your view of a "day in the life of" a salesperson? That by not just knowing the names of the salespeople in other parts of your company, you knew them. Took the time to really connect with them. Grabbed lunch or dinner and, as you would with a prospect or referral source, prepared for that time, came to understand their ambitions and challenges, the things that matter most to them personally. Understood where your interests were aligned, how you could help one another find prospects, how you might be able to collaborate on the same opportunities to create broader solutions, how you could work together on team pitches, or just stay in touch.

Address Conflicts

It's easy to avoid conflict as a salesperson in a large organization. There are a limitless number of workarounds, including working with colleagues you find to be more receptive. Effective teams are able to work through conflicts and disagreements. As you build your network and invest in your internal relationships, what are the odds that between engaged, candid colleagues there will only be moments filled with rainbows and puppy dogs?

Forging larger relationships that span silos works in many ways against the daily momentum within your own organization. It also means creating solutions that don't yet exist as an off-the-shelf capability. That friction can create conflict among colleagues. You may even discover that in working with a colleague from another group for the first time his or her ideas for meeting preparation differ markedly from your own. As a sales and client professional, you resolve objections from clients, prospects, and centers of influence every day. How come it's so easy to get frustrated with our internal colleagues when they don't immediately snap to attention and do what we think they should do? What if we showed the same patience we do with external parties when we are able to resolve their concerns effectively? Instead of ignoring the conflict, what if we acknowledged it, and sought to understand it better before trying to find a way to resolve it? When channel partners are able to know, trust, and work through issues together, imagine how clients view those relationships as they are sizing you up across the table and considering whether to place significant work that involves cross-organization collaboration to deliver it.

Invest in Process

This book is all about going to market as a team, using a team selling-process. Now sales process can differ across disciplines within the same firm. Where one discipline has spent the time to carve out and define a sales process, one uses a different process, and another one uses no process at all. Effective business development professionals use a process—both in shepherding an opportunity over the course of its life, and in managing client touchpoints. It can be frustrating when colleagues with whom they need to work use a different or no process at all.

Teams win together, and teams lose together. Processes that are built on best practices, and applied skillfully and cohesively by a team, will produce consistent results. Random processes or routines produce random outcomes. The team must rally behind a process to win. So how will you close those gaps so the team can be both effective and efficient in its work? We talked earlier about how winning teams work together to resolve conflict; this may be one of those cases. Though we may describe the process around a client meeting in different words, it's tough to imagine anyone disagreeing that this process should include at a high level: time to prepare and practice before the meeting; during the meeting, time allocated to start, discover, present, and end the meeting; and afterward, time to debrief. Establishing expectations at the start sets for members of your selling squad a clear picture of their roles before, during, and after the sales meeting. It allows everyone to visualize, in their own unique way, what that journey looks like.

Create a Feedback Loop

As selling squads come together for important client meetings, the cohesion that is created can form an insular circle that prevents teams from making adjustments needed to win. As an external sales coach, I see—sometimes even within the same organization—widely different examples of feedback cultures. In some groups, feedback comes at you from every angle all the time. In others, it's the Sahara Desert of feedback.

So how do you bridge those gaps to create a feedback exchange with colleagues and business units that you work with today, and those with whom you would like to work in the future? You already understand the importance of keeping your network current and investing in those relationships. You also recognize the importance of working effectively with these colleagues as you team up on selling squads before, during, and after an important client meeting. Effective teamwork includes communicating with one another to help each other maximize your contributions to the team and your impact in the customer meeting.

We have talked about the importance of feedback among selling partners around the selling squad Build Process. We discussed how "P-ER" can be used to develop stronger partnerships through: pre-invest (before the Build Process begins); engage (during the five stages of the Build Process); and re-invest (after the Build Process for a client meeting or pitch is complete. As the team leader in recruiting team members, remember to ask people about their views on and comfort level with feedback. As the group begins to form, set expectations, and gain agreement about when and how feedback will be given, so your colleagues know it will be real feedback, rather than criticism labeled as "feedback." Linking it to the group's performance goal—say, winning a new account that will allow the firm to begin penetrating a high-growth market—makes it feel less personal, and more about a mutual exchange of information intended to allow us to work together more effectively and to win. And a nice by-product of this feedback is that it allows team members to grow individually, and your team, if it works together again, to grow even more effective in future meetings.

Now, let's say you have taken ownership where you are able to. Yet, the organizational climate in which you operate is not conducive to cross-silo teamwork. What actions can you take?

When Your Organization Lacks a Feedback Culture

SEEK COACHING

Many teams get locked into an insular circle where seeking external feedback can feel threatening. Many individuals who work in teams to close business can get so focused on the presentation and the endless number of little activities that lead up to it that the thought of seeking coaching can seem like a time waster. You may also find that, while some leaders within your firm are good coaches, others seem not interested, not available, or not effective at coaching. Yet, taking a step back, you also realize that to produce better and more consistent outcomes as a team leader requires unbiased and skillful coaching. So how do you get it?

There is a short-term answer and a long-term answer to that question. The short-term answer is simple: to seek it out where it exists today and to find coaches who are interested in and skilled at coaching selling squads. Some reside within your company, and some may be available externally. Read on for the long-term answer.

SEEK ORGANIZATIONAL CHANGE

The long-term answer is to seek change. If you and the selling squads you create are not getting the type of coaching you need to get better and win more, your organization needs to hear this from the bottom up, from across your company. Consider taking this on not as a solo crusade, but (naturally) as a team. Who could you include across the organization —now that you have a stronger network, have invested in relationships, and have a belief in process? Who would agree to partner with you to make a case for the availability of more and better coaching? How would that help the broader organization, in addition to your own slice of it, accomplish the goals that have been set?

When do messages communicated by leaders and managers seem to contrast with, for instance, working more effectively together across the firm's disciplines? What if, instead of getting frustrated about the mixed messages you and others are receiving, you consider how to communicate that? This book has equipped you with the tools about how to work effectively as a team in persuading people (customers) in important meetings or pitches. What if, instead, you were trying to persuade a manager, a management team, or a leadership team because you considered this to be a pivotal meeting. What if you took the same approach we have discussed—starting with building a team; prepared feedback that was balanced, specific, and honest; and aligned your team through knowledge leveling, planning, and practice?

On compensation issues, what if you worked together with others to address those areas where the comp program is misaligned with those activities that leadership is seeking and those you know to be essential to winning more in this complex selling environment?

Creating change from the bottom up can be a slow and frustrating process. Just like digging a long tunnel, starting the work from both sides—from your leaders down, and from you and your peers up—will more quickly allow you to meet in the middle and gain the benefits of that new pathway.

CHAPTER 18

NOTES TO SELF

1. Key points to remember about building collaboration in your organization:

   a. _____

   b. _____

   c. _____

2. What actions will you take, and by when, to build collaboration in your organization?

   a. If you're a senior executive or sales manager, leveraging the three C's:

      i. In your communication? _____

      ii. In coaching people and teams? _____

      iii. In compensation? _____

   b. If you're a selling squad leader and/or contributor,:

      i. With your teams? _____

      ii. In your own actions? _____

      iii. Longer term, in your organization?

      _____

CHAPTER 19

CONCLUSION: YOUR COMMITMENTS

Congratulations! By completing this book, you now have a greater appreciation for why selling squads are increasingly called for and the challenges that exist to selling effectively with others. And you have a clearer sense for the process for building a selling squad so you will be able to do it more intentionally and consistently.

You also have reminders or new tools represented in the anchor points below:

- **The four Why's to qualify:** to be sure that you're investing your team's time in the right opportunities
- **P-ER:** pre-invest, engage, and re-invest to build mutually trusting and credible partner relationships
- **The five stages of the selling squad Build Process:** Create, Organize, Practice, Execute, and Re-group
- **The three C's of creating a more collaborative organizational climate:** communication, coaching, and compensation
- **Delivering developmental and deal-team feedback:** as a coach using *How*, *Why*, and *What* questions, and as a peer being balanced, specific, and honest

Whether you're a manager or salesperson, you are walking away with ideas on actions you can take today that will strengthen the conditions for greater teamwork in your organization—today and in the future.

Action Plan

As you've traveled through the pages of this book, you've captured key reminders, actions connected to live opportunities, and priority areas for your own professional development. Now it's time to convert these ideas into an action plan that you are committed to execute. This might take a few minutes, yet it will ensure that you transform what you've learned into the type of results you were seeking when you bought this book.

1. In your own professional development as a senior executive, sales manager, selling squad leader, or contributor, what three takeaways are at the top of your list when you consider how you could drive better and more consistent sales results?
    a.
    b.
    c.
    For each of the items above, be specific about (1) at least one action you will take, (2) what resources (reading, coaching, etc.) will help you, and (3) by when you are committed to completing this action item. (See Figure 19.1.)
2. In regard to an opportunity that you are pursuing, in Figure 19.2 (1) circle the stage of the selling squad Build Process you are in today, and (2) circle those agendas, planners, or knowledge levelers you will leverage to get your team in sync for an upcoming pivotal meeting.

For each of the items circled, be specific about (1) at least one action you will take, (2) what resources (reading, coaching, etc.) will help you, and (3) by when you are committed to completing this action item.

I hope you found this book interesting to read, relevant to your work, and immediately actionable. Now comes the fun part. By committing to

FIGURE 19.1 Your Commitments

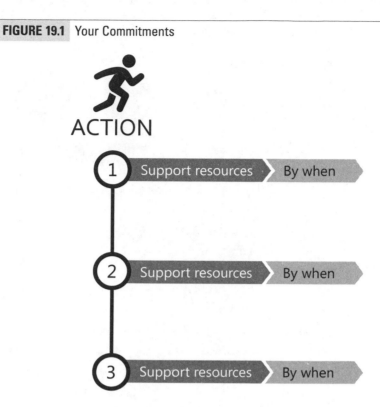

change the way you engage your selling squads and, in turn, strengthening the way your selling squad engages customers and prospects in pivotal meetings, you are putting yourself, your colleagues, and your organization on a better path to win more significant opportunities and to win more frequently.

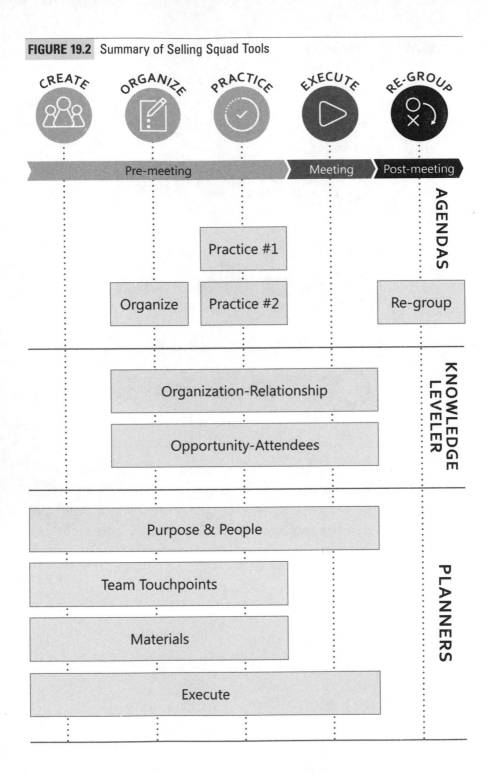

FIGURE 19.2 Summary of Selling Squad Tools

CREATE   ORGANIZE   PRACTICE   EXECUTE   RE-GROUP

Pre-meeting   Meeting   Post-meeting

AGENDAS

Practice #1

Organize   Practice #2   Re-group

KNOWLEDGE LEVELER

Organization-Relationship

Opportunity-Attendees

PLANNERS

Purpose & People

Team Touchpoints

Materials

Execute

BIBLIOGRAPHY

Ariely, Dan, Uri Gneezy, George Loewenstein, and Nina Mazer. "Large Stakes and Big Mistakes." Boston: Federal Reserve Bank of Boston's Research Center for Behavioral Economics and Decision-Making, 2005.

Batamanghelidj, Dr. Fereydoon. "Your Body's Many Cries for Water." Global Health Solutions, 2008.

Bazerman, Max, and Margaret Neale. *Negotiating Rationally*. New York: The Free Press, 1992.

Breskin, David. *We Are the World: The Photos, Music and Inside Story of One of the Most Historic Events in American Popular Music*. New York: Pedigree Books, 1985.

Brown, Daniel James. *The Boys in the Boat: Nine Americans and Their Epic Quest for Gold at the 1936 Berlin Olympics*. New York: Penguin Books, 2013.

Bryant, Adam. "Lars Dalgaard: Build Trust by Daring to Show That You're Human." *New York Times*, October 17, 2015. http://www.nytimes.com/2015/10/18/business/lars-dalgaard-build-trust-by-daring-to-show-that-youre-human.html?_r=0.

Cainey, Andrew, Frans Blom, and Gunther Schwarz. "The Three Golden Rules of Cross-Selling." White Paper: The Boston Consulting Group, 2002.

Coffey, Wayne. *The Boys of Winter: The Untold Story of a Coach, a Dream, and the 1980 U.S. Olympic Hockey Team*. New York: Three Rivers Press, 2005.

CSO Insights. 2015 Sales Performance Optimization Study. Boulder, CO: CSO Insights, 2015.

Dalis, Michael. "5 Tips on How to Use a Subject Matter Expert in a Sales Meeting." *HubSpot* (blog), July 21, 2015. https://blog.hubspot.com/sales/how-to-use-a-subject-matter-expert-in-a-sales-meeting#sm.0001f0eildoace8qxb01rq71awofp.

Dalis, Michael. June 2015. "Interview with Sandy Dalis."

Dalis, Michael. August 6, 2015. "Interview with Brent Carter."

Dalis, Michael. August 7, 2015. "Interview with Evan Weinstein."

Dalis, Michael. Auguest 11, 2015. "Interview with Raymond Rodriguez."

Dalis, Michael. "5 Tips on How To Use a C-Level Executive in a Sales Meeting." *HubSpot* (blog), April 30, 2015. https://blog.hubspot.com/sales/tips-on-how-to-use-a-c-level-executive#sm.0001f0eildoace8qxb01rq71awofp.

Dalis, Michael. *Teamwork in Selling*. Philadelphia, PA: The Richardson Company, 2015.

Dalis, Michael. "How's Your Selling Energy?" *Richardson* (blog), February 19, 2014. http://blogs.richardson.com/2014/02/19/hows-selling-energy/.

ESPN. "E:60, Silent Night Lights." 2015.

Fisher, Roger, and William Ury. *Getting to Yes: Negotiating Agreement Without Giving In*. New York: Penguin Books, 2011.

Fernández-Aráoz, Claudio. "How to Make a Team of Stars Work." *Harvard Business Review,* July 17, 2015.

Gardner, Heidi. "Coming Through When It Matters Most." *Harvard Business Review,* April 2012.

Gardner, Heidi. "Performance Pressure as a Double-Edged Sword: Enhancing Team Motivation While Undermining the Use of Team Knowledge." Working Paper, Boston, MA: Harvard Business School, 2012.

Gardner, Heidi. "When Senior Managers Won't Collaborate." *Harvard Business Review*, March 2015.

Glucksberg, Samuel. "The Influence of Strength of Drive on Functional Fixedness and perceptual recognition." *Journal of Experimental Psychology*, 1962, pp. 36–41.

Greenleaf, Robert K. *Servant Leadership: A Journey Into the Nature of Legitimate Power and Greatness*. New York: Paulist Press, 1977.

Hackman, Richard. *Leading Teams: Setting the Stage for Great Performances*. Boston: Harvard Business School Publishing, 2002.

Hanson, Ben, Kurt Schroeder, and Kate Woelffer. "Solve the Cross-Selling Puzzle: Customer Experience Is the Missing Piece." White Paper: Baker Tilly, 2014.

Katzenbach, Jon R., and Douglas K. Smith. *The Discipline of Teams: A Mindbook-Workbook for Delivering Small Group Performance*. New York: John Wiley & Sons, 2001.

Katzenbach. Jon R., and Douglas K. Smith. *The Wisdom of Teams*. Boston: Harvard Business School Press, 1993.

Kotter, John P. *Leading Change*. Boston, MA: Harvard Business Review Press, 2014.

LaFasto, Frank, and Carl Larson. *When Teams Work Best: 6,000 Team Members and Leaders Tell What It Takes to Succeed*. Thousand Oaks, CA: Sage Publications, 2001.

Larson, Carl, and Frank LaFasto. *TeamWork: What Must Go Right/What Can Go Wrong*. Newbury Park, CA: SAGE Publications, 1989.

Lencioni, Patrick. *The Five Dysfunctions of a Team: A Leadership Fable*. San Francisco: Jossey-Bass, 2002.

Mankins, Michael C., Alan Bird, and James Root, "Making Star Teams Out of Star Players." *Harvard Business Review*, January–February 2013.

Marketing Leadership Council. "The Digital Revolution in B2B Marketing." Arlington, VA: Corporate Executive Board, 2012.

McChrystal, General Stanley. *Team of Teams: New Rules of Engagement for a Complex World*. New York: Portfolio/Penguin, 2015.

Moon, Mark, and Gary Armstrong. "Selling Teams: A Conceptual Framework and Research Agenda." *Journal of Personal Selling & Sales Management*, Winter 1994, pp. 17–30.

Moorman, Michael B., and Chad Albrecht. "Team Selling: Getting Incentive Compensation Right." *Velocity*, Q2 2008, pp. 33–37.

National Sleep Foundation. "What Happens When You Sleep?" Accessed December 2015. https://sleepfoundation.org/how-sleep-works/what-happens-when-you-sleep.

Pentland, Alex. *Honest Signals: How They Shape Our World*. Cambridge, MA: MIT Press, 2008.

Pentland, Alex. "The New Science of Building Great Teams." *Harvard Business Review*, April 2012.

Pentland, Alex. *Social Physics: How Social Networks Can Make Us Smarter*. New York: Penguin Books, 2014.

Perkins, Dennis N.T., and Jillian B. Murphy. *Into the Storm: Lessons in Teamwork from the Treacherous Sydney to Hobart Ocean Race*. New York: AMACOM Books, 2013.

Richardson, Linda. *Stop Telling, Start Selling: How to Use Customer-Focused Dialogue to Close Sales*. New York: McGraw-Hill, 1998.

Richardson, Linda. *Winning Group Sales Presentations: A Guide to Closing the Deal*. Homewood, IL: Dow Jones-Irwin, 1990

Salesforce. 2015 State of Sales Report. San Francisco, CA: Salesforce Research, 2015.

Steiner, Ivan. 1972. *Group Process and Productivity*. Cambridge, MA: Academic Press Inc., 1972.

Stone, Douglas, and Sheila Heen. *Thanks for the Feedback: The Science and Art of Receiving Feedback Well*. New York, NY: Penguin Group, 2014.

Thalheimer, Will. "How Much Do People Forget?" A Work-Learning Research Document. December 2010.

Weil, Dr. Andrew. "Three Breathing Exercises." Accessed December 2015. http://www.drweil.com/drw/u/ART00521/three-breathing-exercises.html.

Weisinger, Hendrie, and J.P. Pawliw-Fry. *Performing Under Pressure: The Science of Doing Your Best When It Matters Most*. New York: Crown Business, 2015.

Wheelan, Susan A. *Creating Effective Teams: A Guide for Members and Leaders*. Thousand Oaks, CA: Sage Publications, 2010.

Wilson, Ernest J. III. "Empathy Is Still Lacking in the Leaders Who Need it Most." hbr.org. September 21, 2015. https://hbr.org/2015/09/empathy-is-still-lacking-in-the-leaders-who-need-it-most.

Wooden, John, and Jay Carty. *Coach Wooden's Pyramid of Success: Building Blocks for a Better Life*. Ventura, CA: Regal Books, 2005.

Woolley, Anita Williams, Christopher Chabris, Alex Pentland, et al. "Evidence for a Collective Intelligence Factor in the Performance of Human Groups." *Science*, 29 October 2010, pp. 686–688.

ACKNOWLEDGMENTS

This book is the product of my experiences and, consistent with the title, contributions from valued friends and colleagues.

I am grateful to the clients, prospects, and advisors I served, for helping me learn what worked for you and what didn't. I hope you experienced more and more of the former, and less and less of the latter.

I would like to thank my colleagues at State Street Global Advisors and State Street Bank that I supported, led, and/or coached during my years there. From you, I learned what it takes to be a leader and teammate on teams that win.

To my friends from the High School of Performing Arts, from whom I learned so much as a young man, I continue to admire and learn from you about performance discipline.

I thank my trusted friends and readers for the generosity of their time and the wisdom of their feedback on my early drafts. In particular, I'm grateful to Ginger Schlanger, Susan Raynes, Henri Barber, Irv Grossman, and Lawrence Dalis, my dad. Your observations challenged my thinking and no doubt made this a more useful book to more people.

To the leadership team and my colleagues at The Richardson Company, thank you for your partnership and support on this project and the excellent work you do every day to increase sales effectiveness around the world; I am proud to represent you.

A special thank you to Linda Richardson, who redirected me when I was stuck and got me moving in the right direction.

Thanks also to my new friends at McGraw-Hill. Especially to Donya Dickerson, for her persistence in keeping this project on track. And to Amy Li, for her deft touch during the editing process.

And, finally, thanks to Sandy Dalis, my wife, reader, best friend, and health coach. You listened, pushed, guided, loved, and understood me, always at the right time. This project was possible and worthwhile only because of you.

INDEX

Note: Page numbers followed by *f* refer to figures.

ABOUT THE AUTHOR

Michael Dalis has for more than 30 years been a successful salesperson, sales leader, and sales coach. Starting out as a commercial banker, he shifted to the institutional investment business, where he became a managing director responsible for driving rapid growth in a new channel at one of the world's largest investment management companies. Today he is a senior consultant for The Richardson Company, a global leader in ensuring sustained behavior change driving increased sales performance. He specializes in leading skills-based workshops for companies in the financial and professional services sectors. He also provides deal coaching to select companies through DRIVE Sales Consulting. Michael is a dedicated runner and has completed several ultramarathons. He lives in California with his wife, Sandy, and their Great Pyrenees, Lily, and he is the proud father of daughter, Melissa.